Michael E. Burnette

Emotional Intelligence and the Police

D1296212

Michael E. Burnette

Emotional Intelligence and the Police

Do Patrol Sergeants Influence the Emotional Intelligence of their Subordinate Officers?

VDM Verlag Dr. Müller

Imprint

Bibliographic information by the German National Library: The German National Library lists this publication at the German National Bibliography; detailed bibliographic information is available on the Internet at http://dnb.d-nb.de.
     Any brand names and product names mentioned in this book are subject to trademark, brand or patent protection and are trademarks or registered trademarks of their respective holders. The use of brand names, product names, common names, trade names, product descriptions etc. even without a particular marking in this works is in no way to be construed to mean that such names may be regarded as unrestricted in respect of trademark and brand protection legislation and could thus be used by anyone.

Cover image: www.purestockx.com

Publisher:
VDM Verlag Dr. Müller Aktiengesellschaft & Co. KG
Dudweiler Landstr. 125 a, 66123 Saarbrücken, Germany
Phone +49 681 9100-698, Fax +49 681 9100-988, Email: info@vdm-verlag.de

Produced in USA and UK by:
Lightning Source Inc., La Vergne, Tennessee, USA
Lightning Source UK Ltd., Milton Keynes, UK

ISBN: 978-3-8364-3473-7

ABSTRACT

BURNETTE, MICHAEL EDD. The Relationship Between Emotional Intelligence of Patrol Sergeants and Subordinate Patrol Officers. (Under the direction of Audrey J. Jaeger and Don C. Locke.)

This research project was undertaken to investigate the relationship between the emotional intelligence levels of patrol sergeants and the emotional intelligence levels of their respective subordinate patrol officers. Given the nature of the policing, the potential benefit to law enforcement agencies employing officers with functional or high levels of emotional intelligence was assumed to be a desirable attribute. Contributions to the research literature was considered a worthy endeavor regarding the correlation of patrol sergeants' emotional intelligence as it may be correlated to the emotional intelligence of the sergeants' subordinate officers.

This study was assisted by a law enforcement agency in the Southeastern United States to derive the population sample. After failing to acquire participation from a sufficient randomly selected sample from the population, a convenience sample was derived and data were collected from 22 sergeants (96%) and 82 officers (54%). Bar-On's Emotional Quotient Inventory (EQ-i) was used to acquire the emotional intelligence scores of the participating sergeants and officers.

Data analysis was conducted using the Pearson product-moment correlation to determine if a linear correlation existed between the patrol sergeants' EQ-i scores and the EQ-i scores of their respective subordinate officers. The results of this analysis determined that no statistically significant correlation existed between the independent variables of the Sergeants Total EQ-i and five Composite scores and the dependent variables of the Patrol Officers Total EQ-i and five Composite scores. A t-test was also instituted to analyze the mean score differences between the groupings of patrol sergeants and patrol officers. The results of this test yielded no statistically significant differences between the respective groups. Based upon the statistical results of the study, the null hypothesis was retained.

Recommendations were suggested that included 1) the use of an abilities-based EQ-i test instrument for future research, 2) the use of experiments within the ranks of supervisors and field training officers to determine if enhancement of emotional intelligence will have a quantifiable effect on subordinate personnel, 3) the use of emotional intelligence enhancement training to reduce police burnout and occupational stress, and 4) the use of and participation in emotional intelligence research projects directed toward the policing profession.

DEDICATIONS

To my wife, Janet

my daughter, Hannah

my son, Kevin

and to the memory of

Dr. Byrdie E. Eason

1934 - 2005

And we know that all things work together

for good to them that love God,

to them who are the called

according to his purpose.

Romans 8:28 (KJV)

ACKNOWLEDGEMENTS

During this "doctoral journey," I have developed an immense appreciation and gratitude for the concern, commitment, knowledge, and support of numerous individuals, for whom without their support, I would never have begun the "journey" and most certainly would have never completed it.

I wish to recognize and thank my committee members, Dr. Audrey Jaeger (Co-Chair), Dr. Don C. Locke (Co-Chair), Dr. Thomas E.H. Conway, Jr., and Dr. Janice Odom for the generous sharing of their time, knowledge, and expertise in this dissertation process. The direction and guidance offered by Dr. Audrey Jaeger, whose expertise in the field of emotional intelligence, has been of epic importance to the completion of this project. The encouragement, inspiration, and challenges provided by Dr. Don C. Locke, Professor Emeritus – NCSU, current Director of Diversity and Multicultural Affairs of UNC-A, and former Director of the Asheville Graduate Center, leaves me personally indebted to him for life. I wish to also thank Dr. Robbie Pittman for his excellent instruction and assistance in completing the statistical analysis of this project.

I would like to also thank the members of the Asheville "Trihort" for their friendship, encouragement, and support during this sometimes-arduous "journey." In particular, I would like to thank Drs. David Shockley, Keith Mackie, Gary Davis, Jeni Wyatt, and Russ Foster as well as Carol Burton, Lorene Putnam, and Carrie Gates for helping make this journey an enjoyable one because it was shared with close friends and academic colleagues.

I would also like to acknowledge the assistance provided to me by the law enforcement officers and supervisors who participated in this study. Without their direct involvement in this project, I would never have been able to collect data and ultimately report my findings in this dissertation.

Most especially, I wish to convey my heartfelt love and deepest appreciation to my wife, friend, and mentor, Janet. I sincerely appreciate all your assistance, love, and unconditional sacrifices in helping me complete this "journey." I am also tremendously blessed to have Hannah, who has sacrificed playtime with Daddy so that I could work on various projects during the past four and one half years. I hope to be able to reciprocate this love and support by being available for her throughout her life and educational endeavors. I also wish to thank my son, Kevin, who has patiently listened to and talked to me about my "journey" each Wednesday evening for three years. I also wish to thank my mother, Joyce Burnette, for her encouragement and support throughout my entire life and academic career.

During this research process, the memory of my father, Edd Burnette, has been a constant reminder and inspiration to me. Throughout my childhood and on into adulthood, my father continually expressed to me through both word and deed that "anything worth doing is worth doing right." I now presume that he was helping prepare me for this doctoral "journey."

TABLE OF CONTENTS

x

LIST OF TABLES

LIST OF FIGURES

CHAPTER ONE

INTRODUCTION

There are, perhaps, few occupations in our nation that can bring about a cacophony of emotional responses more quickly than law enforcement personnel. Each of us can identify a feeling of pride and honor remembering the heroic efforts of New York City police officers rushing into the World Trade Center's Twin Towers, accompanying brave fire fighters, in an effort to save lives only to lose their own on September 11, 2001. In almost the same moment, we can summon mental images to remind us of the brutality of a Los Angeles police sergeant and three other officers beating Rodney King in 1992.

"No quality is more indispensable to a policeman than a perfect command of temper; a quiet, determined manner has more effect than violent action" (Bohm & Haley, 2005, p. 150) wrote Sir Robert Peel, Home Secretary of England, on defining one of the twelve principles of policing derived from the Metropolitan Police Act of 1829. A major aspect of the rapidly emerging field of emotional intelligence is an emphasis on one's ability to regulate one's emotions. Clearly, the two precepts are related and it may be that emotional intelligence is a concept with great potential for application in the law enforcement arena.

Law enforcement personnel regularly deal with stressful and emotionally charged issues as they perform the duties of their respective offices. How they respond to these circumstances can range from heroic to repugnant. It is the contention of this researcher that emotionally intelligent law enforcement supervisors play a significant role in leading by example and thereby impacting how their subordinate patrol officers will respond in stressful circumstances. Law enforcement administration practitioners and scholars (Bennett & Hess, 2004; More & Wegener, 1996) indicate that effective law enforcement departments have an integral thread woven into the fabric of the agency: high-quality patrol supervisors. Harrison (2001) stated

> Although some may minimize the impact of the sergeant's role, it is the most important level of management; they are the ones who implement philosophy and turn intent into reality. Their work will either motivate or discourage those around them... They alone view, monitor and interact with those who are performing the core functions of policing (p. 151).

Are police officers in the field being provided proper guidance by line supervisors? Does field supervision of patrol officers really matter? In response to the latter question, Engel (2003) provided a qualified "yes." Her research indicated the style or quality of field supervision has a greater influence on patrol officers than the quantity of supervision.

In recent years, researchers (Abraham, 1998; Ashkanasy & Dasborough, 2003; Bardzil & Slaski, 2003; Barling, Slater, & Kelloway, 2000; Boyatis & Oosten, 2002; Brooks, 2002; Buford, 2001; Carmeli, 2003; Caruso & Salovey, 2004; Cherniss & Adler, 2000; Cherniss & Caplan, 2001; Cherniss & Goleman, 2001; Cooper & Sawaf, 1997; Feldman, 1999; Gardner & Stough, 2002; George, 2000; Goleman, 1998; Higgs & Aitken, 2003; Langley, 2000; Johnson & Indvik; Massey, 1999; Møller & Powell, 2001; Palmer, Walls, Burgess, & Stough, 2001; Rahim & Minors, 2003; Rozell, Pettijohn, & Parker, 2002; Sivanathan & Fekken, 2002; Stubbs, 2005; Weinberger, 2003; Wong & Law, 2002) have explored the influence of emotional intelligence on managers within organizations. These researchers have presented empirical findings that suggest appropriate training in emotional intelligence may have substantial benefits for improving the supervisor's concern for quality and problem solving. Emotional intelligence has been examined as a measure for identifying how effective leaders monitor and respond to their subordinates (Palmer, Walls, Burgess & Stough, 2001).

Statement of the Problem

Historically, within law enforcement personnel agencies, the responsibility of patrol supervisors or patrol sergeants has included traditional functions of managing patrol activities, collecting reports, maintaining discipline and compliance to rules and regulations, and investigating incidences involving their subordinate patrol officers (Bennett & Hess, 2004). The notion that law enforcement personnel supervisory styles can and may influence the patrol officer has been examined by a National Institute of Justice study conducted by Mastrofski, Parks, Reiss and Worden (1999, 1998). The conclusions garnered from this research reveal that law enforcement personnel supervisors can influence the behavior and attitudes of their subordinates (Engel & Worden, 2003).

Emotional intelligence has been defined as "a cross-section of interrelated emotional and social competencies, skills and facilitators that determine how effectively we understand and express ourselves, understand others and relate with them, and cope with daily demands" (Bar-On, 2005, p.3). This construct provides an avenue to evaluate the relationship of emotional intelligence between police supervisors and their subordinate officers.

The need to identify emotional intelligence competencies in prospective candidates for employment in police work should be a consideration made by police administrators during the hiring process. Jacobs (2001) provided a specific model for emotional intelligence competencies that should be ascertained in helping and human service workers, such as the police, which include principles of self-control, empathy, teamwork and collaboration, conflict management, and communication. Bar-On (1997) identified a stress resistance (SR) component of emotional intelligence that would have direct bearing on law enforcement supervisors' and officers' abilities to function effectively and carry out the duties of their respective positions.

Given this background, emotional intelligence may possibly become an important factor for use in evaluating law enforcement supervisors. Research addressing the role of emotional intelligence in law enforcement has been limited to two studies (Bar-On, Brown, Kirkcaldy, & Thomé, 2000; Ricca, 2003); one comparing the emotional intelligence scores of police officers, child-care workers, and social workers and the other examining efforts to reduce police burnout. Due to the paucity of empirical studies regarding this subject, researchers and practitioners are limited in their ability to consider the influence of emotional intelligence as a means of assessing performance, hiring, promoting, and training law enforcement personnel.

Emotional intelligence has been examined as a factor contributing to the discussion of leadership effectiveness. There exists significant research regarding the relationship of emotional intelligence and leadership effectiveness. However, the studies (Ashkanasy & Dasborough, 2003; Barling, Slater, & Kelloway, 2000; Brooks, 2002; Buford, 2003; Carmeli, 2003; Cherniss & Adler, 2000; Cooper & Sawaf, 1997; Feldman,

1999; Gardner & Stough, 2002; George, 2000; Goleman, 1998; Hartsfield, 2003; Langley, 2000; Johnson & Indvik, 1999; Massey, 1999; Møller & Powell, 2001; Palmer, Walls, Burgess, & Stough, 2001; Schulte, 2003; Sivanathan & Fekken, 2002; Stubbs, 2005; Weinberger, 2003; Wong & Law, 2002) reported contradicting conclusions regarding the influence of emotional intelligence and leadership effectiveness.

Due to the lack of inquiry and literature published regarding the relationship between a law enforcement supervisor's level of emotional intelligence and the subordinate officer's level of emotional intelligence, it appears that this research would be a beginning in an attempt to fill this void. However, the true value of this research could be directed toward providing the law enforcement community a valuable tool to assist police administrators in screening for and hiring the best candidate as well as enhancing current officers' abilities to function more effectively within their respective communities.

Purpose of the Study

The purpose of this study is to investigate the relationship between the emotional intelligence levels of patrol supervisors and the emotional intelligence levels of their subordinate patrol officers. The results will potentially be of value to the law enforcement agency involved in the study and may also have implications for other law enforcement agencies.

Research Questions

The research question which will drive this study is as follows:

1.   Is there a relationship between the emotional intelligence level of the

patrol supervisor and the emotional intelligence level of the subordinate

patrol officer?

Definitions

For the purpose of this study, the following definitions will apply:

Emotional intelligence is "a cross-section of interrelated emotional and social

competencies, skills and facilitators that determine how effectively we understand and

express ourselves, understand others and relate with them, and cope with daily demands"

(Bar-On, 2000, p.3).

EQ-i refers to the Emotional Quotient Inventory created by Reuven Bar-On

(2000) as an experimental instrument in the early 1980's. Bar-On describes the EQ-i "as

a self-report measure of emotionally and socially competent behavior that provides an

estimate of one's emotional and social intelligence" (p. 364).

Law enforcement or *law enforcement officer* refers to any governmental officer

with arrest powers in a specific geographic jurisdiction. The terms *law enforcement* or

law enforcement officer or patrol officer are used interchangeably with the terms *police*

or *police officer*.

Line sergeant refers to any sergeant who has direct supervisory responsibilities

for a number of patrol officers within his or her jurisdiction. The term is used

interchangeably with *patrol supervisor*.

Patrol officer refers to any law enforcement officer who has arrest powers and is charged with the responsibility of enforcing the laws of a particular state or jurisdiction. This term is used interchangeably with *law enforcement or law enforcement officer or police or police officer.*

Patrol supervisor refers to any sergeant who has direct supervisory responsibilities for a number of patrol officers within his or her jurisdiction. The term is used interchangeably with *line sergeant.*

Police or *police officer* refers to any governmental officer with arrest powers in a specific geographic jurisdiction. The terms *police* or *police officer* are used interchangeably with the terms *law enforcement* or *law enforcement officer or patrol officer.*

Assumptions

The following assumptions are made regarding this study:

1. Sergeants and patrol officers will honestly respond to all questions posed in the Emotional Quotient Inventory (EQ-i) test instrument.

2. Emotional intelligence can be measured using the Bar-On EQ-i instrument for both line sergeants and patrol officers.

Limitations

The following limitations are applied to this study:

1. The line sergeants involved in this study will be of varying ages and will also have varying levels of experience in law enforcement and supervision.

8

8

2.   The officers involved in this study will be of varying ages and will also have varying levels of experience in law enforcement.

3.   The results of this study will not be generalizable beyond the population of this study.

4.   There exist other commercially available, emotional intelligence assessment instruments; however, the EQ-i has been selected as the assessment instrument to be used in this study.

5.   The Bar-On EQ-i is a self-reporting instrument.

6.   All participants have voluntarily agreed to take part in this study.

7.   The data collection sample is a convenience sample.

Significance of the Study

Law enforcement agencies across the state and the nation are continually challenged to hire the best-qualified applicants for the job of policing. Failure to properly hire, train, and supervise a law enforcement officer can result in civil liability actions entangling the officer, the supervisor, the department, and the governing body (Adams, 2004; Hess & Wrobleski, 1997; Peak, 2004). In today's litigious society, failure to properly train and failure to properly supervise law enforcement officers are the two most frequent civil actions brought against supervisors, departments, and their governing bodies (Hess & Wrobleski, 1997).

Given the gravity of these actions, law enforcement agencies would be well advised to look for tools and resources which can assist in properly hiring, training, and supervising their officers. The results of this study may potentially identify a measure which could mitigate claims of negligent hiring and promoting, insufficient training and improper supervision on the part of a supervisor, department, or governing body. Additionally, the results of this study could demonstrate that emotional intelligence enhancement training of patrol supervisors would increase the emotional intelligence levels of subordinate patrol officers in the field.

The results of this study will enrich the bodies of literature and research involved in the fields of criminal justice administration, adult education, and organizational psychology. The findings will be valuable in the support of future research in these fields, with particular emphasis on the value of emotional intelligence to criminal justice administrators.

CHAPTER TWO

LITERATURE REVIEW

Introduction

Law enforcement supervisors and the officers they supervise have been scrutinized, evaluated, and tested in one format or another for almost a century. Termin and Otis (1917) used the Stanford-Binet intelligence scale to test police officers in San Jose, California. They determined that an intelligence quotient of approximately 80 was the minimum acceptable level for police officers to be able to discharge the duties of their office.

Today, Dade County (FL) police candidates are required, as part of the application process to become a police officer, to take the Florida Basic Abilities Test (F-BAT). This test attempts to evaluate 16 abilities ranging from deductive reasoning to written expression that should indicate an applicant's ability to perform the duties of a sworn police officer (Miami Dade College, 2005). Jacksonville (FL) Sheriff's Office also requires a battery of pre-employment tests for police officers. These include: 1) physical agility test, 2) writing skills test, 3) polygraph exam, 4) background investigation, 5) oral review board interview, 6) medical/stress test, 7) drug screen, and 8) psychological exam (Jacksonville Sheriff's Office, 2005).

State police agency candidates are also subjected to many testing hurdles in the pre-employment process as well. Candidates must successfully complete the following tests in order to be accepted for employment with these agencies. The tests may include: 1) vision test, 2) physical fitness test, 3) written test, 4) polygraph examination, 5) background investigation, 6) applicant review board, 7) physical examination, and

8) psychological test.

Testing is a requisite part of promotional activities within law enforcement agencies as well. Many state police agencies require officers desiring promotion to line sergeant to complete a series of tests. The process may be delineated as: 1) the candidate will successfully complete an internally developed policy and law exam; 2) the candidate will successfully complete a pre-supervisor video presentation and test; 3) the candidate will successfully complete the phase one certification board which includes practical application exercises and a scenario-based case analysis; and 4) the top 50 candidates must successfully complete the phase two certification board which involves interactive job scenarios and a panel interview.

As indicated by the plethora of testing procedures, law enforcement recruits are assessed and analyzed prior to employment in an effort to find the ideal officer who is suited for the demands of the job and who will be willing to commit to a long-term career in law enforcement (Bennett & Hess, 2004). Given the extensive testing process to select law enforcement officers in many departments across the nation, especially the psychological test administered to candidates, it would appear that incidences of police brutality and abuse of power would be completely eradicated or significantly limited to an infinitesimal rate of occurrence. Recent history and experience has taught us that this is not the case and it would therefore appear intuitive to test in order to determine the emotional intelligence levels of these prospective officers as a means of reducing these persistent and sometimes pervasive problems within the nation's constabulary.

Jacobs (2001) offered a compelling argument for identifying emotional intelligence competencies in prospective candidates for employment. She provided a specific model for emotional intelligence competencies to be ascertained in helping and

human service workers which include competencies of self-awareness, social awareness,

self-management, and social skills as depicted in Figure 1. Emphasis is placed on the

bolded competencies.

Self Awareness	Social Awareness
• Emotional Self-Awareness or **Accurate Self-Assessment** • **Self Confidence**	• **Empathy** • Organizational Awareness or **Service Orientation**
Self-Management	Social Skills
• **Self-Control** • Trustworthiness or Conscientiousness or Adaptability • Achievement Orientation or **Initiative**	• **Influence** • Leading Others or **Developing Others** • Building Bonds or **Teamwork and Collaboration** or **Conflict Management** • Communication or Change Catalyst

Figure 1. Emotional Intelligence Competence Model for Helping and Human Service
Workers
Note. From *The Emotionally Intelligent Workplace: How to Select for, Measure, and
Improve Emotional Intelligence in Individuals, Groups, and Organizations,* (p. 170), by
C. Cherniss and D. Goleman, 2001, San Francisco: Jossey-Bass. Copyright 2001 by
Cary Cherniss and Daniel Goleman. Reprinted with permission.

Additionally, Jacobs (2001) developed a model for emotional intelligence

competencies in supervisory personnel. These competencies are exactly the same as described in the model for helping and human service workers; however the emphasis is

on the bolded competencies in each cluster as illustrated in Figure 2.

Self Awareness	Social Awareness
• Emotional Self-Awareness or Accurate Self-Assessment • **Self Confidence**	• **Empathy** • **Organizational Awareness** or Service Orientation
Self-Management	Social Skills
• **Self-Control** • **Trustworthiness** or Conscientiousness or Adaptability • **Achievement Orientation** or Initiative	• **Influence** • **Leading Others** or **Developing Others** • Building Bonds or Teamwork and Collaboration or **Conflict Management** • **Communication** or Change Catalyst

Figure 2. Emotional Intelligence Competence Model for Managers

Note. From *The Emotionally Intelligent Workplace: How to Select for, Measure, and Improve Emotional Intelligence in Individuals, Groups, and Organizations,* (p. 167), by C. Cherniss and D. Goleman, 2001, San Francisco: Jossey-Bass. Copyright 2001 by Cary Cherniss and Daniel Goleman. Reprinted with permission.

Incorporation of emotional intelligence competencies appears to provide a new

dimension for exploration in the context of human resource acquisition and development in the policing profession. It is a desire of this literature review to explore the continuum of thought, theory, and ideology concerning emotional intelligence and its possible application to law enforcement officers.

The purpose of this literature review is to a) research the history and development of emotional intelligence theories, b) research the application of emotional intelligence in organizations, c) research the relationship of the emotional intelligence of a police supervisor and his or her employee, and d) examine the application of emotional intelligence to law enforcement front line supervision.

Intelligence Theories

Historical Overview

Civilized society has recognized and understood a distinction regarding human intelligence and its byproduct, knowledge, for centuries. Aristotle made specific reference to knowledge in his treatise *On the Soul* (Aristotle, trans.1931). Plato wrote about the question posed by Socrates to Meno regarding the acquisition of knowledge:

> And if there have been always true thoughts in him, both at the time when he was and was not a man, which only need to be awakened into knowledge by putting questions to him, his soul must have always possessed this knowledge, for he always either was or was not a man? (Plato, trans. 1871).

For centuries, humankind maintained a tacit understanding of intelligences or capacities held by various individuals that were expressed in different venues. Sun Tzu and Julius Caesar were considered to be military geniuses; Mozart was considered to be a musical genius and Michelangelo an artistic genius. It was not until the beginning of the

20th century an attempt was actually made at establishing and measuring quantitatively an individual's mental capacity or intellect.

In an editorial published posthumously, Robert Thorndike (1994) indicated the first practicable version of human intellect assessment was made available for scholarly critique almost a century before. Thorndike also alluded to the fact that Spearman's (1904) general ability factor or "g" was first theorized during the beginning of the 20th century as a construct of general intelligence.

Argument and dissent encompassed much of the early literature regarding the validity presented by theorists propounding the views of a "general intelligence" and the capacity of psychologists to measure it. Terman (1922) stated "There is nothing about an individual as important as his IQ" and to that end he was required to suffer Lippmann's stinging reproach:

> The claim that we have learned how to measure hereditary intelligence has no scientific foundation. We cannot measure intelligence when we have never defined it, and we cannot speak of its hereditary basis after it has been indistinguishably fused with a thousand educational and environmental influences from the time of conception to the school age. The claim that Mr. Terman or anyone else is measuring hereditary intelligence has no more scientific foundation than a hundred other fads, vitamins and glands and amateur psychoanalysis and correspondence courses in will power, and it will pass them into that limbo where phrenology and palmistry and characterology and the other Babu sciences are to be found. In all of these there was some admixture of primitive truth which the

conscientious scientist retains long after the wave of popular credulity has spent

itself (Lippmann, 1922, p. 213).

It is evident that acrimony and academic rancor have proliferated in the discussion of

intelligence and the means for measuring it.

Definitions of Intelligence

Early attempts to define and quantify cognitive intelligent was initiated at the

beginning of the 20th century by researchers like Spearman and Terman et.al. Spearman

(1904) deduced four distinct classifications of intelligences: 1) present efficiency or

ability to perform well in classic studies, 2) native capacity or the individual's class

ranking in relationship to his or her age, 3) general impression or the impression made by

the individual on others as to whether he or she was bright, average or dull, and 4)

common sense or the individual's ability to understand and properly react to

circumstances outside of academia. This construct established his definition of general

intelligence or "g." Terman et.al. (1917) defined intelligence as the ability to carry on

abstract thinking. The views of these scientists were restrictively directed toward the

examination of an individual's quantifiable cognitive abilities which were assigned a

numeric ranking and obligatory assessment of mental acuity or lack thereof.

Other theorists agreed that one's cognitive ability was an important part of an

individual's intelligence but believed that there was more to the concept of intelligence.

E.L. Thorndike (1920) divided intelligence into three specific components of 1) *abstract*

intelligence which is the ability to conceptualize ideas, 2) *concrete intelligence* or the

cognitive ability to understand and then act upon that understanding, and 3) *social*

intelligence which is the ability to understand people and to interact with them wisely.

Wechsler (1958, 1974) continued Thorndike's theoretical perspective of intelligence being more than one's cognitive ability by broadening his definition and stating that "intelligence is the aggregate or global capacity of the individual to act purposely, to think rationally, and to deal effectively with his environment" (1974, p.32). Wechsler (1974) surmised "that general intelligence cannot be equated with intellectual ability however broadly defined, but must be regarded as a manifestation of the personality as a whole" (p.39).

Toward the end of the 20th century another theorist considered the definitions of intelligence and prescribed similar attributions to the concept of intelligence which had previously been derived. Gardner (1993) indicated that "intelligence is defined operationally as the ability to answer items on tests of intelligence" (p.15). Gardner (1983, 1993) however, propounded a new notion regarding intelligence when he developed the construct of multiple intelligences.

The concept of intelligences other than cognitive intelligence has survived a cyclic process of acclaim and ambiguity over the years and has been resurrected at various times during the 20th century in an attempt to further understand human intelligence. One of those resurrections has been directed at the body of knowledge identified as social intelligence.

Social Intelligence

It would appear that many persons of science implicitly understood the concept of social intelligence; however, Thorndike appears to be the first to actually acknowledge it as a component of human intellect and capacity. E. L. Thorndike (1920) wrote that there were for "ordinary practical purposes, however, it suffices to examine for three 'intelligences,' which we may call mechanical intelligence, social intelligence, and abstract intelligence" (p. 228). He expounded upon social intelligence as being "the ability to understand and manage men and women, boys and girls – to act wisely in human relations" (p. 228).

As previously mentioned, social intelligence has maintained a "roller coaster" existence in the theoretical constructs of the scientific community. An explanation for this cyclic subsistence of social intelligence may be found in Walker and Foley's work. In 1973, Walker and Foley considered the aspect of the cyclic nature of social intelligence and its measurement. They reviewed eight tests which were created over a period of 30 years and purported to measure social intelligence with varying levels of validity and reliability. Cronbach (1970) also contributed to this explanation with his opinion expressed in this statement, "After fifty years of intermittent investigation, however, social intelligence remains unidentified and unmeasured" (p.319).

In the most recent years, researchers, practitioners, organizations and individuals have realized that social intelligence is constructed of multiple competencies that are attributed to a person's ability to interact with others. This perspective is, according to social intelligence research, directly related to the cultural context an individual may find himself or herself. Topping, Bremner, and Holmes (2000) explored the concept of social competencies as it related to social intelligence. They define social competence as the "ability to integrate thinking, feeling, and behavior to achieve social tasks and outcomes valued in the host context and culture" (p.32). Based upon the cultural component variable discussed by Topping, Bremner, and Holmes (2000), it would appear that the police culture may directly affect the way and manner in which the police think, react and behave (Bar-On, Brown, Kirkcaldy, & Thomé, 2000; Lord, 1996; Pogrebin and Poole, 1991; Ricca, 2003; Savery, Soutar, and Weaver, 1993).

Social intelligence and social competencies appeared to provide a transition to the conceptualization of multiple intelligences which allows an individual the opportunity to express him or herself in a manner that is recognized as a form of intelligence separate and apart from cognitive ability.

Multiple Intelligences

The idea that an individual was invested with more resources than cognitive ability has not been a new revelation of thought. However, considerable study and inquiry regarding the concept of multiple intelligences has received considerable attention, particularly during the latter portion of the 20th century. Gardner brought to bear an aspect of consideration that humankind has multiple means, at its disposal, of considering a person's capacity to think, respond, act, and produce intellectual potentials beyond the parameter of cognitive ability. Gardner (1983) indicated he does not disagree with the concept of general intelligence; however, he opines that it is a constituent of a far broader group of intelligences of which he theorizes to be multiple intelligences. Gardner (1993) refined his definition of intelligence as "the ability to solve problems or fashion products that are of consequence in a particular cultural setting or community" (p. 15). Gardner (1983) advanced the concept of multiple intelligence which "posits a small set of human intellectual potentials, perhaps as few as seven in number, of which all individuals are capable by virtue of their membership in the human species" (p. 278). Gardner (1999) extended the seven intelligences to eight by adding the naturalist in his taxonomy of multiple intelligences.

With Gardner enhancing the body of knowledge surrounding multiple intelligences, Sternberg (1985) postulated a triarchic view of human intelligence. This theory divides human intelligence into three domains: componential, experiential, and contextual. Towers (1988) expounded upon these three domains by explaining the *contextual perspective* constitutes the traditional intelligence measured by IQ tests; the *experiential perspective* translates to the individual's external experiences mediated by the internal mental process and how the individual's internal mental process changed the external experiences; and the *contextual perspective* represents the individual's adaptability to the environment.

Multiple intelligences allow the postulation of a new construct of intelligence. This new theory of intelligence embodies the idea that the intrapersonal and interpersonal aspects of multiple intelligences and social intelligence provides a nexus to consider an individual's emotional intelligence as a part of the defining composition of who that person is and how they relate to other members of society.

Emotional Intelligence

Origins of Emotional Intelligence

The concept of emotional intelligence appears to have been an evolutionary process from the concepts of social intelligence first postulated by E. L. Thorndike in 1920 and advanced by Laird in 1925 and Moss et.al. in 1927 (Teschler, Biberman & McKeage, 2002). Thorndike defined social intelligence as "the ability to understand men and women, boys and girls – to act wisely in human relations" (p. 228). Wechsler (1958) expounded upon Thorndike's perspective by indicating that social intelligence is a "...facility in dealing with human beings" (p. 8).

Progressing on the path of discovery toward a defining of emotional intelligence, Gardner (1983, 1993) posited the concept that individuals possess multiple intelligences and ultimately opened the door for advancing the idea of personal intelligences and eventually the concept of emotional intelligence. Gardner (1999) proposed eight intelligences including interpersonal and intrapersonal intelligences. Interpersonal intelligence turns outward with the core capacity or "ability to notice and make distinctions among other individuals and, in particular, among their moods, temperaments, motivations, and intentions" (p. 239). Intrapersonal intelligence turns inward with the core capacity or "access to one's own feeling life – one's range of affects or emotions: the capacity instantly to effect discriminations among these feelings and, eventually, to label them, to enmesh them in symbolic codes, to draw upon them as a means of understanding and guiding one's behavior" (Gardner, 1983, p. 239).

Sternberg's (1985) triarchic theory went beyond the conventional and traditionalist views of intelligence relating only to cognitive abilities and presents a methodology for measuring or operationalizing social and practical intelligence. Sternberg (1985) illustrated his three contextual sub-theories, which included analytical (componential), creative (experiential), and practical (contextual) facets of human intelligence. Steinberg's (1985) theory was established primarily by observing Yale graduate students and he believed that properly defining and measuring intelligence could translate into real-life success. Sternberg also discussed four categorizations of knowledge that are associated with social and practical intelligence in the real-world that may lead to occupational successes in many fields: 1) knowing how to manage people;

2) knowing how to manage tasks; 3) knowing how to manage self; and 4) knowing how to manage career (Sternberg, 1985, p. 270).

Emotional intelligence was formed by intertwining the constructs of social intelligence and multiple intelligences. Salovey and Mayer (1990) were the first to theorize the construct and coin the term "emotional intelligence." This construct's components consisted of: 1) the ability of appraising one's own emotions and expressing those emotions to others effectively; 2) the skill of recognizing emotional responses in others, empathetically gauging the proper affective response, and choosing the most socially adaptive behavior in response; 3) the ability of regulating and enhancing one's own mood and the moods of others thereby motivating others toward the accomplishment of a particular goal or end; and 4) the ability of solving problems adaptively by integrating emotional considerations when choosing alternatives to a particular problem or issue.

Emotional intelligence was introduced to the global community and business world as a predictor of successful interpersonal relations between individuals which would ultimately impact the success of organizations around the world. Goleman (1995) popularized the term emotional intelligence and brought it before the mass media and business world as "the underlying premise for all management training" (1998, p. 8). Goleman (2001) clarified his position that emotional intelligence will emerge as a stronger predictor than IQ in distinguishing successful people within a particular job category or profession. Although Goleman's views, definitions, and models have a significant appeal to the lay person, they lack the scientific rigor necessary to advance them to the point of establishing a theoretical construct.

Once a theory is developed the next logical step to advancing that theory is to contrive a means of measuring the construct. Emotional intelligence was advanced to the level of having a viable means of measuring a set of variables. Bar-On's (1997a, 2000, 2005) model constituted the first self-reporting, peer-reviewed testing procedure of its kind measuring emotionally and socially intelligent behavior. The test provided a quantitative estimate or score of five composite scales comprised of fifteen subscales that will be described in detail later in this review. The model is established on the theoretical basis that "emotional-social intelligence is a cross-section of interrelated emotional and social competencies, skills and facilitators that determine how effectively we understand and express ourselves, understand others and relate with them, and cope with daily demands" (Bar-On, 2000, p. 3).

Over time, two other models for measuring emotional intelligence were constructed. Schutte and his colleagues (Schutte, Malouff, Hall, Haggerty, Cooper, Golden, et.al., 1998) developed the self-report Emotional Intelligence test (SREIT) which is described as a brief self-report measure of an individual's emotional intelligence. It consisted of 62 self-report items that were primarily based on Salovey and Mayer's (1990) early model of emotional intelligence, which composed one's ability to monitor and discriminate emotions and to use emotions to guide one's thinking and actions (Brackett & Mayer, 2004). Mayer, Salovey and Caruso developed the Multifactor Emotional Intelligence Scale in 1999 and refined it into its present iteration, the Mayer-Salovey-Caruso Emotional Intelligence Test, Version 2.0 (MSCEIT V2.0). The MSCEIT V2.0 was tested regarding its validity and reliability in 2002. It was intended to measure four branches, or skill groups, of emotional intelligence: a) perceiving emotion accurately, b) using emotion to facilitate cognitive activities, c) understanding emotion, and d) managing emotion (Mayer, Salovey, Caruso, & Sitarenios, 2004).

Following the significant acceptance (Bar-On & Parker, 2000) of Goleman's (1995) book entitled *Emotional Intelligence*, organizations began to consider the application of emotional intelligence in the workplace by enhancing the emotional intelligence of current employees and the selection of potential employees (Goleman, 1998). Cherniss (2001) indicated that emotional intelligence plays a significant role in organizational effectiveness. He contended that those organizations with supervisors who manage with emotional intelligence are perceived to be more trustworthy, empathetic, and caring by their subordinates. According to Cherniss (2001), emotionally intelligent organizations and managers are more capable of recruiting, retaining, and developing talented employees within those organizations. Cherniss (2000) expressed a concern regarding the rapid changes that are effecting organizations today and indicated that greater demands will be placed on the manager and employee's cognitive, emotional and physical resources. He advocated that a person's emotional intelligence will become an increasingly valuable asset by improving productivity and psychological well-being within the workplace. Although the insights expressed by Cherniss and his colleagues (Cherniss, 2001; Cherniss, 2000; Cherniss & Adler, 2000; Cherniss & Caplan, 2001) regarding emotional intelligence in the workplace appear to be very clear and cogent, they fail to directly support their assertions with valid research data. It appears that these works tend to be more illustrative guides for the practitioner rather than grounded in scientific research.

Defining Emotional Intelligence

Being a multifaceted construct, emotional intelligence tends to make the task of defining it difficult. A number of definitions have been proposed; however, there tends to be substantial differences in each of them and they do not tend to mesh well with each other.

Salovey and Mayer (2004) first coined the term 'emotional intelligence' in 1990 by defining it as "the subset of social intelligence that involves the ability to monitor one's own and others' feelings and emotions, to discriminate among them and to use this information to guide one's thinking and actions" (p. 5). Mayer and Salovey (2004) indicated their original definition was vague and impoverished and therein revised and expanded the definition of emotional intelligence. The revised and expanded definition is:

> Emotional intelligence involves the ability to perceive accurately, appraise, and express emotion; the ability to access and/or generate feelings when they facilitate thought; the ability to understand emotion and emotional knowledge; and the ability to regulate emotions to promote emotional and intellectual growth (Mayer & Salovey, 2004, p. 35).

The next definition of emotional intelligence is established by Goleman as an introduction to the mass media regarding this concept. Goleman (1995) introduces, in *Emotional Intelligence*, his definition of emotional intelligence that appealed to the average person as an understandable and cogent explanation of this new term that had gained entry into the American vernacular. Although well written for advancing an understanding of emotional intelligence to the lay person, Goleman's work appeared to lack credible scientific validity other than the work of others that he occasionally cited. Goleman (1998) defined emotional intelligence as "the capacity for recognizing our own feelings and those of others, for motivating ourselves, and for managing emotions well in ourselves and in our relationships" (p. 317). Goleman (1995) also identified, in his model of emotional intelligence, five basic emotional and social competencies: 1) self-awareness, 2) self-regulation, 3) motivation, 4) empathy, and 5) social skills.

The final definition presented is that of Bar-On (2005). He defined emotional-social intelligence as "a cross-section of interrelated emotional and social competencies, skills and facilitators that determine how effectively we understand and express ourselves, understand others and relate with them, and cope with daily demands" (p.3). Bar-On (1997, 2005) also developed the Emotional Quotient Inventory (EQ-i) providing the first published, peer-reviewed, and quantifiable measure or score of an individual's emotional intelligence level.

Emotional Intelligence in Organizations

Overview of EI in Organizations

Change within an organization is an absolute. According to Katz and Kahn (1978), the general systems theory of organizations has in place a universal law of nature indicating a failure to change on the part of the organization will eventually cause entropy which, in turn, will ultimately led to its disorganization and death. Burke (2002) states that more than 95% of organizational change is evolutionary; organizations respond to the need to change by making small, incremental steps toward improving functionality.

Today's police organizations appear to be on the threshold of change both technologically and philosophically in order to function effectively in the 21st century

(Anderson, 2000). Change regarding the way and manner in which the police deal with the citizens they are sworn to serve and protect will, to which the general systems theory is stipulated, have to occur and this change may require an enhancement of the police officer's interpersonal skills. This will possibly convey a new means of evaluation and assessment for police officers and police organizations.

Do organizations concentrate primarily on an individual's skills, intellectual capacity, or job knowledge in order to determine their value to the organization and ultimate success within the organization? Goleman (1998) discussed a new "yardstick" for measuring people within an organization. Kotter and Cohen (2002) indicated that "people change what they do less because they are given analysis that shifts their thinking than because they are shown a truth that influences their feelings" (p. 1). Cherniss and Adler (2000) stated that emotional intelligence matters more now than ever in the context of adapting to change. In the wake of massive changes occurring in the American and global workplace, brought about by technical innovation, global competition and investment pressures, personal qualifications or competencies of initiative, resilience, and optimism may be needed by current and potential employees to insure organizational success.

With emotional intelligence being considered a formidable measure for enhancing organizational effectiveness, Abraham (1998) conceptualized and posited nine empirically testable propositions for imbuing emotional intelligence into an organization's infrastructure (see Table 1).

Table 1

Propositions for Emotional Intelligence in an Organization's Infrastructure

Emotional intelligence is directly related to work-group cohesion.

Emotional intelligence moderates the congruence between self and supervisor ratings during job performance feedback.

Emotional intelligence is directly related to organizational performance.

Emotional intelligence is directly related to organizational commitment.

Emotional intelligence is directly related to employees exerting more effort on behalf of the organization or enhancing organizational citizenship.

Emotional intelligence decreases emotional dissonance related to job satisfaction and organizational commitment.

Emotional intelligence may either increase or decrease job dissatisfaction and organizational commitment related to ethical role conflict by employees.

Emotional intelligence causes employees to suffer less job insecurity and less erosion of organizational commitment even in the light of short term job contracts.

High job control by employees, or the freedom to implement change by the employee, allows emotional intelligence to increase organizational commitment within employees.

Note. Adapted from Abraham, 1998.

As demonstrated by Abraham's propositions, emotional intelligence has the potential to directly contribute to and increase benefits for organizations employing emotionally intelligence employees. Researchers and practitioners have indicated that in order to accomplish a change in the organization it becomes necessary to establish a direct link to a perceived need for the members of the organization to 'buy-in' and see the impact of their role in the organization in order to bring about change (Boyatzis & Oosten, 2002; Cherniss & Caplan, 2001; Kotter & Cohen, 2002).

In order to effectively operate an organization with emotionally intelligent employees is it necessary to have them directed by emotionally intelligent supervisors? Johnson and Indvik (1999) elucidated the benefits to an organization that employs intelligent managers and employees. They proclaimed in organizations where emotional intelligence is present the organizations' profitability increased due to the inextricable link between the trust and loyalty within the organization which translated into a higher quality of work life for the employee.

Is it necessary to have emotionally intelligent people in all aspects of an organization? According to Wong and Law (2002) there are indications that hiring only highly emotionally intelligent employees may be a waste of resources unless the job requires a high degree of emotional intelligence in order for the employee to function effectively. They continue by describing the issue of 'emotional labor' as "the extent to which the job requires the management of emotions to achieve positive job outcomes and study the moderating effects of emotional labor on the EI-job outcome relationships" (Wong & Law, 2002, p. 248). Their hypothesis indicated the effects of emotional intelligence on job outcomes will not be the same across job categories and is thereby regulated by the emotional labor attached to each job. Results of three studies conducted by Wong and Law (2002) validated this hypothesis. Research by Brooks (2002) may possibly corroborate the findings by Wong and Law. Brooks indicated that higher levels of emotional intelligence were not related to higher levels of job performance in her sample. As we may ascertain from this discussion, the enhancement of an individual's job performance and effectiveness by emotional intelligence may certainly be dependant upon the necessity of interaction with others based upon the individual's particular job assignment. However, when individuals come together within an organization and are required to interact with each other in order to accomplish a team goal the need for emotional intelligence within the group is exponentially increased by the number of individuals in that specific group.

Group Emotional Intelligence

Do human emotions collectively grow out of social interaction with others? Does this social interaction within organizational work groups need to be effectively managed by using emotional intelligence in order to produce successful results within the group? Druskat and Wolff (2001a) introduced the concept of group emotional intelligence (GEI) and defined it as "the ability to develop a set of norms that manage emotional processes so as to cultivate trust, group identity, and group efficacy" (p. 133).

Emotional intelligence can augment a group's cohesion and goal attainment by increasing the group members' abilities to communicate, foster understanding, and empathy for their colleagues' welfare. Rahim and Minors (2003) expounded on Goleman's (1995, 1998) five competencies model for emotional intelligence which include: a) Self-awareness, b) Self-regulation, c) Motivation, d) Empathy, and e) Social skills; by developing a 35-item instrument to measure them. In particular, there are two competencies that appear to be very important to the discussion of relationship building, empathy, and social skills.

Empathy refers to understanding and development of others, a service orientation toward the welfare of others, a move toward leveraging diversity and political awareness. *Social skills* are explained as those skills and abilities that are directly associated with influence, communication, conflict management, leadership, change catalyst, building bonds, collaboration and cooperation and team building

capabilities (Rahim & Minors, 2003, p. 150).

Rahim and Minors' (2003) research yielded a relatively low response (22.2%)

from the randomly selected population of 1,000 Chamber of Commerce members. The

results of the study provided partial support of Goleman's five emotional intelligence

components. The researchers acknowledged the limitations of their study to be a low

response rate and the presence of common method variance in the measures which very

likely inflated the correlations established in their findings (Rahim & Minors, 2003, p.

154).

Being capable of understanding emotions within groups is an essential component

for the models created to predict group behavior and thereby manage a powerful

influence over the group. Ultimately, groups that are emotionally intelligent will be

capable of developing a sense of group self-awareness and an ability to group self-

regulate (Druskat & Wolff, 2001a, 2001b). In order to increase better decisions, more

creative solutions, and higher productivity within an organization, Druskat and Wolff

(2001b) emphasized the establishing of three basic conditions within the group. These

three conditions include: 1) mutual trust among all group members, 2) a sense of

belonging to the group of all members of the group, and 3) a belief that there exists a

synergistic effect within the group and that the group is capable of achieving more

working together than working apart. Druskat and Wolff (2001b, p.154) created an

impressive model for explaining how group emotional intelligence influences

cooperation and collaboration; however, they fall short in providing a mechanism to facilitate and test their model. Lacking this test mechanism subjects their postulations to little more than supposition and speculation.

Williams and Sternberg (1988) initiated the conceptualization of group intelligence by establishing that the characteristics of the group are important to internal harmony and maximization of productivity. Their study considered both the cognitive skills or IQ and social skills of the collective group and concluded that the groups with the maximum values for creativity, diversity, practicality of ideas, and IQ were therefore the groups with the highest level of group intelligence. The study was conducted as an experimental process that examined 96 subjects who were divided into four conditions and then placed in groups of three same-gender persons per group. The groups were presented with two problems that they solved based upon the group condition imposed by the experimenters. The findings demonstrated that group products were significantly better than individual products. Multiple regression on group product quality demonstrated Beta values on all variables measured to be at a statistical significance level of $p < .05$, $p < .01$, or $p < .001$ (Williams & Steinberg, 1988, p. 373). The value of this study is significant to the understanding of group dynamics and group emotional intelligence.

Group or team emotional intelligence must foster an environment that is conducive to building strong interpersonal and group relationships that strive toward a common purpose and objective. Goleman (1998) advocated that in order to build highly effective teams, team members must exhibit a talent for social coordination. He expounded upon this concept by indicating three competencies for social coordination: 1) building bonds by nurturing instrumental relationships, 2) collaborating and cooperating by working together toward the accomplishment of shared goals, and 3)

creating a synergy in working toward group goals.

The "emotional contagion" effect (Caruso & Salovey, 2004) may be used as an

effective and strategic tool by emotionally intelligent leaders to motivate people toward a

common goal and can also positively or negatively affect the group's emotional state.

Kelly and Barsade (2001) discussed the impact of the emotions of one individual being

transferred to the group in what was referred to as emotional contagion. If one member

of the group is excited, elated, depressed, or angry, the emotional impact may be felt by

everyone in the group, particularly if that individual expresses those emotions to the

group.

Can emotional intelligence control the group's emotional state and enhance their

performance in a variety of circumstances? Yost and Tucker (2000) conducted a study

regarding team emotional intelligence in a junior level college course of 73

predominately business majors that were divided into 19 teams for analysis. Reported

results positively correlated the independent variable of emotional intelligence to the

dependent variables of team performance, problem solving, and project grade. Based

upon the statistical significance of the results of this study suggesting that emotionally

intelligent teams are more effective in areas of higher problem-solving capabilities; it

may be tentatively assumed that the results could be replicated within a police

organization with similar results. The three vexing issues associated with this study are

the 1) relatively small sample size, 2) lack of randomization in the study subjects, and 3)

use of a convenience sample of college students ranging in ages from 19 -25 years.

Moriarty and Buckley (2003) demonstrated by use of group processes to build team skills, resolve internal differences, and accomplish group goals, that members of the experimental group enhanced their emotional intelligence levels significantly within the experimental group from the pre-test to post-test intervals. This research used a valid experimental design with a control and experimental group; however, the subjects of this study were college students. A contention raised twice by the researchers in their findings was that the experimental group surpassed the control group in the post-test analysis. The researchers acknowledged that their findings did not reach a level of statistical significance necessary to validate their hypothesis; yet they appeared to contend that the experimental group experienced an increase in emotional intelligence that superseded the increase of the emotional intelligence level of the control group. The statistical data from the study did not bear this contention out.

An interesting question surfaced with many of the studies presented in this literature review: Do college students represent a peer sample for working police officers and can the results derived from these studies be inferred to a police organization? It becomes very apparent that the lack of research studies involving police organizations and emotional intelligence magnifies the necessity of such research.

If group emotional intelligence actually exists as a theoretical construct then a method for validly and reliably measuring group emotional intelligence is required to demonstrate its efficacy. Druskat and Wolff (2001) argued that three conditions are essential to a group's effectiveness. The conditions are: 1) trust among members, 2) a sense of group identity, and 3) a sense of group efficacy. Based upon Druskat and Wolff's conceptualization of group emotional intelligence, Hamme (2003) developed an assessment instrument to measure group emotional intelligence with a total of ten reliable subscales. The apparent usefulness of this particular instrument appeared to be significant; however, there are no studies indicated in the body of literature that illustrated this contention other than Hamme's (2003) study.

According to Champion (2003), work group cohesiveness is an important part of job satisfaction for the police officer. An officer who has a good relationship with his or her work group and is well integrated into the work group will be a happier and more productive officer in comparison to one who is not integrated into the work group (p. 162). In an examination of 159 Canadian police managers and supervisors, group cohesiveness or social nearness was reported to generate higher levels of job satisfaction despite the perceived stress of the job (Perrott & Taylor, 1995).

In recent years a new emphasis has been placed on organizations with respect to stress management, conflict resolution, diversity, responsive leadership and effective teamwork (Bassi, 1996). Due to these changes in organizations, it is not surprising that the ability of employees to become engaged in dialogue and communication within and between groups has cited emotional intelligence as a cornerstone for organizational growth and productivity (Massey, 1999).

It becomes evident that a means of measuring group emotional intelligence is needed to document and determine the validity and reliability of speculation regarding the benefit of group emotional intelligence. Jordan, Ashkanasy, Härtel, and Hooper (2002) initiated a study that employed the Workgroup Emotional Intelligence Profile, Version 3 (WEIP-3) which was specifically designed to profile the emotional intelligence of individuals in work groups. The methodology used by this study engaged the participation of 448 Australian undergraduate students enrolled in a managerial skills and communication course over a 14-week semester. Analysis of the results (2002) indicated that relative to their study, low emotional intelligence groups do not perform well in comparison to high emotional intelligence groups; however, over time the low emotional intelligence groups may perform as well as high emotional intelligence groups. After completing the study, the researchers could not make a definite conclusion regarding the reason for this improvement. The researchers established both convergent and discriminant validity with their test instrument using five other valid test instruments. The results indicated that the WEIP-3 was a valid instrument for application in this study.

This research was compelling in that the high emotional intelligence teams seemed to have the requisite skills to perform well relative to goal focus and process criteria and the low emotional intelligence teams appeared to lack these skills. Jordan, Ashkanasy, Härtel, and Hooper (2002) indicated a number of factors that could have possibly produced these contrary findings. The supposition of the researchers included training, familiarity with other team members, or dominant team members emerging whose individual skills improved the performance of the team.

Moriarty and Buckley (2003), using Jordan's et.al. refined WEIP-5, concluded that training a group in emotional intelligence responses established skills that allow team members to understand their own styles of emotional interactions, handle emotions in the workplace, and increase their individual level of self-awareness and self-concept. The outcome of these positive skills enhanced both the individual human potential and group potential thereby benefiting the organization.

Emotional Intelligence and Organizational Leadership

In order to fully integrate emotional intelligence into an organization is it necessary that the organization be lead by emotionally intelligent executives and managers? Caruso and Salovey (2004) maintained that emotions at work influence judgment, job satisfaction, helping behavior, creative problem solving, and decision making. Caruso and Salovey (2004) also indicated managers can use emotions to influence their subordinates in accomplishing the goals of the organization by correctly matching the mood or emotion to the moment. Managers with high emotional intelligence can achieve results from their subordinates that are synergistic in nature and are far superior to normal expectations (Johnson & Indvik, 1999). Cooper and Sawaf (1997), Salovey and Shuyter (1997), and Goleman (1998) suggested that emotional intelligence is a core essential for effective leadership. The question can then be postulated for inquiry; is the manager's high emotional intelligence the catalyst that creates this synergy to allow subordinates to achieve the higher than normal expectations or could there be other causative factors?

Do emotionally intelligent leaders have the capacity to effectively appraise emotions and emotional environments as well as use emotions effectively to influence others? George (2000) elucidated the four major aspects of emotional intelligence that contribute to effective leadership within organizations (see Table 2).

Table 2

Emotional Intelligence Factors Contributing to Effective Leadership

The appraisal and expression of emotion in self and others

The use of emotion to enhance cognitive processes and decision making in self and others

The comprehension of knowledge regarding emotions in self and others

The management of emotions in self and others

Note. Adapted from George, 2000.

The supposition of how emotional intelligence can contribute to effective leadership within an organization may possibly be answered by five fundamental statements outlined in an article written by Jennifer George (2000). She presented five elements wherein emotional intelligence may enhance a leader's abilities and performance:

1. Effective and emotionally intelligent leaders establish a vision or mission for the organization and then clearly communicate to his or her subordinates a collective sense of the goals necessary to accomplish this vision or mission and the viable objectives to achieve the goals by being able to assess their subordinates' emotions and influence their receptivity to the vision.

2. Effective and emotionally intelligent leaders are capable of instilling in others an appreciation of the importance of their work activities and at the same time raise the subordinates' confidence levels in their ability to overcome problems and meet challenges by subtly managing their own emotions and the emotions of their subordinates.

3. Effective and emotionally intelligent leaders generate and maintain excitement, enthusiasm, confidence and optimism in the organization while at the same time engendering cooperation and trust in their subordinates by developing high quality, interpersonal relationships with their subordinates.

4. Effective and emotionally intelligent leaders encourage flexibility in decision making and change by accurately perceiving their own emotions and include them in the equation of decision making as well as perceiving the emotions of their subordinates and thereby effectively overcome their resistance and influence change within their subordinates and ultimately their organization.

5. Effective and emotionally intelligent leaders inculcate and maintain a meaningful organizational identity contained within their subordinates by evoking an emotional affirmation of the values that are consistent with the organization's culture (George, 2000).

Organizational leaders must confront the issue of interpersonal relationships within their respective organizations. Disagreements, misunderstandings, and failures to effectively communicate can result in dysfunctional relationships and internal quagmires for organizational leaders. Does the organizational leader truly act in an emotionally intelligent manner to resolve these issues or does he or she merely pay 'lip service' to the concept of emotional intelligence and the positive influence it may have in difficult circumstances? Bolman and Deal (1997) discussed the interpersonal dynamics in an organization where "many of the greatest joys and most intense sorrows occur in relationships with other people" (p.144). Interpersonal competence or effectiveness is controlled by personal theories for action: espoused theories or theories-in-use.

Espoused theories are used when a person attempts to describe, explain, or predict their behavior. Theories-in-use are the implicit rules that constitute what the person actually does. Most often there are significant discrepancies between the espoused theories and theories-in-use. In order for emotional intelligence to be effective and not just another passing fad, senior administration, mid-level supervisors, front line supervisors, and employees within the organization must 'buy-in' in order to sustain a long term effect (Cherniss, 2000; Cherniss & Adler, 2000; Cherniss & Caplan, 2001; Goleman, 1998, 2001).

The benefits of emotional intelligence are not instantaneous. Organizational executives, mid-level managers, and front line supervisors must commit to instilling the concepts of emotional intelligence within the core of the organization. Kram and Cherniss (2001) concluded that there exists a significant gap between the espoused declaration of support for innovative training programs such as emotional intelligence by senior management within an organization and the realistic action that may actually take place within the organization looking for immediate results. Emotionally intelligent leaders will direct their subordinates by example and establish values and trust that transcend immediacy of short term profits or productivity (Caruso & Salovey, 2004; Cherniss & Caplan, 2001; George, 2000; Goleman, 1998; Langley, 2000; Rahim & Minors, 2003).

Effective leaders, according to Sivanathan and Fekken (2002), demonstrate a capacity for making good judgments and this is empirically related to moral reasoning and emotional intelligence. Police officers often find themselves at a crossroad for making appropriate moral judgments and applying emotionally sound reasoning in their jobs. In reality, no other person in the criminal justice system has the opportunity to utilize discretion more often than the patrol officer. The patrol officer has the power and authority to determine who receives a verbal reprimand, who receives a citation, who goes to court, who goes to jail, who gets hurt or, in extreme circumstances, who gets killed. The responsibility to make the best judgment call resides within that particular officer at that particular time. Will he or she effectively utilize moral reasoning and emotional intelligence to make the best decision? Lives could be inextricably changed forever if the officer lacks emotional intelligence and a capacity for appropriate moral reasoning.

Emotionally intelligent leaders must sustain a high level of personal integrity in order to establish the trust and cooperation of their subordinates. Cooper and Sawaf (1997) expounded upon Yale law professor Stephen L. Carter's three core characteristics of personal integrity regarding emotional intelligence and the effective leader.

The first criterion is the ability to discern what is right and what is wrong which is reflected in emotional intelligence as a degree of moral reflectiveness. The second criterion is the ability to act on what you have discerned, even at a personal cost of career, success, or even life. The third and final criterion is the ability to say openly that you are acting on your understanding and belief of right from wrong, yet still be willing to temper this with compassion (Cooper & Sawaf, 1997, p. 166).

Emotionally intelligent leaders must also be capable of acknowledging and overcoming negative affective states within themselves in order to induce a positive affective state in their subordinates. A leader's emotional state can direct either a positive or negative "emotional contagion" within the organization (Caruso & Salovey, 2004). This emotional phenomenon is neither intelligent nor unintelligent; however, it can be strategically applied by the emotionally intelligent leader. Carmeli (2003) expanded upon Salovey and Mayer's (1990) conceptually-related mental process of regulating emotion in one's self and others. He indicated that by regulating your own emotions into a positive affective state you will be able to experience negative affective states without potentially destructive consequences. He also provided this thought; "Emotionally astute people can induce a positive affect in others that results in a powerful social influence..." (Carmeli, 2003, p. 791).

Organizational leaders may be capable of transformational leadership wherein they motivate their followers to perform beyond expectations by intellectually stimulating and inspiring them to transcend their own self-interest for a higher collective purpose (Sivanathan and Fekken 2002). This transcendence requires the leader to exhibit an ability to communicate openly and honestly with his or her subordinates in order to accomplish the organizational tasks at hand.

Are emotionally intelligent leaders just transformational leaders in a new and improved packaging? It appears from the literature review that emotionally intelligent leaders may, in fact, use transformational techniques in order to effect change within their organization and motivate their subordinates. Barling, Slater, and Kelloway (2000) presented arguments related to why leaders high in emotional intelligence would be more likely to use transformational behaviors than leaders with lower emotional intelligence levels. First, leaders with high emotional intelligence could serve as role models for their subordinates by demonstrating and displaying an ability to manage their own emotions and delay gratification. Second, leaders with high emotional intelligence would be very capable of realizing the extent to which they would be able to inspire their subordinates. Third, leaders manifesting emotional intelligence would be capable of effectively managing empathetic relationships with their subordinates. These perspectives clearly demonstrate transformational behaviors that influence, inspire, intellectually stimulate, and motivate followers (Bass & Avolio, 1994). A study conducted by Palmer, Walls, Burgess and Stough (2001) using the Trait Meta Mood Scale (TMMS) instrument developed by Salovey, Mayer, Goldman, Turvey, and Palfai in conjunction with the Multifactor Leadership Questionnaire (MLQ) created by Avolio, Bass, and Jung hypothesized that transformational leaders would be higher in emotional intelligence than transactional leaders. The results of their study did not reveal evidence sufficient enough to support their hypothesis; however, they discovered that "inspirational motivation and individualized consideration components of transformational leadership were significantly correlated with both the ability to monitor and manage emotions in one's self and in others" (Palmer, Wall, Burgess, & Stough, 2001, p. 8).

Emotional Intelligence between Supervisors and Subordinates

The literature provides an abundance of anecdotal advice on the development of emotional intelligence in organizations as well as the advancement and proliferation of emotional intelligence training for supervisors and subordinates (Abraham, 1998; Ashkanasy & Dasborough, 2003; Bagshaw, 2000; Barling, Slater, & Kelloway, 2000; Boyatzis & Oosten, 2002; Brooks, 2002; Caruso & Salovey, 2004; Cherniss, 2001; Cherniss & Adler, 2000; Cherniss & Caplan, 2001; Feldman, 1999; George, 2000; Goleman, 2001; Goleman, 1998; Jacobs, 2001; Kram & Cherniss, 2001; Langley, 2000;

Johnson & Indvik, 1999; Massey, 1999; Møller & Powell, 2001; Palmer, Burgess, & Stough, 2001; Sivanathan & Fekken, 2002); many of these works lack the supporting, foundational research needed to advance the authors' views. The literature does provide several interesting studies offering valid research which advances the idea that a link may exist between the emotional intelligence of supervisors and subordinates (Barling & Slaski, 2003; Buford, 2001; Carmeli, 2003; Gardner & Stough, 2002; Higgs & Aitken, 2003; Rozell, Pettijohn, & Parker, 2002; Weinberger, 2003; Wong & Law, 2002).

Stubbs (2005) presented research demonstrating that a team leader's emotional intelligence will influence the development of group level emotional intelligence. Results of her study concluded that a team leader's emotional intelligence is significantly related to the presence of emotionally competent group norms of the teams that he or she may lead and that these norms are related to team performance. Data were collected from 81 teams within a military organization. The similarities between the organizational structure of military and police organizations (Adams, 2004; Bennett & Hess, 2004; Champion, 2003) may provide an interesting backdrop for future research into the emotional intelligence of police supervisors and their subordinate officers.

Emotional Intelligence and Law Enforcement Supervision

Theories of Law Enforcement Organization and Supervision

Police organizations have not, based upon an extensive literature search, developed and implemented any unique theories of organizational structure, management or leadership. Most organizational and leadership theories employed by the police, according to Anderson (2000) have emerged from business and academia.

Police leadership evolved along the business management paradigm. Much like the business model, police management was searching for a more effective means of directing and managing police personnel. Peak (2004) presented the historical approach to police management as being divided into three distinct approaches which are as follows: 1) scientific management (1900-1940), 2) human relations management (1930-1970), and 3) systems management (1965-present). Originating from these management styles were several management models and leadership theories. Among these were the bureaucratic model, the goals model, the decision model (Champion, 2003), contingency models and behavioral models (Stojkovic, Kalinich, & Klofas, 1998), McGregor's Theory X and Theory Y, Likert's Four-System Approach theory, Blake and Mouton's Leadership Grid theory, and Argyris' Mature Employee theory (Bennett & Hess, 2004), Ouchi's Theory Z, and Alderson's Theory R (Anderson, 2000).

Understanding the various leadership theories used by police agencies over time assists in conceptualizing the motivation of police executives to accomplish specific goals. Anderson (2000) has done a thorough job encapsulating an overview of traditional theories of leadership used by police professionals over the years. He presented the biological personality theories as including the Great Man Theory and trait theories. Both of these theories, although in question, advanced the notion that certain people are born stronger, more intelligent, and with an innate capacity to lead and govern others. These characteristics or traits are biologically-based and can not be learned. Anderson also discussed the environmental theories that cause great leaders to rise to the occasion. He articulated the personal-situational theories that proposed a complex set of factors that were responsible for shaping and developing leaders as well as the theoretical orientations that leadership is the act of initiating and fulfilling the expectations of followers (Anderson, 2000).

Although emotional intelligence has not yet been considered to be a humanistic theory of police leadership, the antecedent theories explored and expounded upon created a direct connection to this theory. Anderson (2000) focused on the humanistic theories of leadership that allow the organizational employee to meet his or her personal needs and the organizational objectives at the same time. He also considered the situational or contingency theories of leadership reflecting the belief that there is a relationship between employees' satisfaction and performance and their environment. If we are able to understand the factors that influence employee morale and adjust the leader's response to these factors, we may be able to impact productivity and possibly public service orientation in the policing profession.

Summary of Leadership Theories

Westberg (1931) proposed that critical factors involved in leadership were a combination of the "affective, intellectual, and action traits of the individual as well as the specific conditions under which the individual operates" (p.420). This conceptualization advances the premise that successful leadership is accomplished by the leader's ability to understand the subordinates and the surrounding environment and react appropriately to those situations as they change. Bennis (1961) recommended that leadership should constitute a measure of rationality including a consideration for the impact of informal organizational and interpersonal relationships, job enlargement and employee-centered supervision that permits individual self-development, participative management and joint consultation in allowing the integration of individual and organizational goals. He emphasized the value of the person in relationship to productivity as well as importance of the interpersonal dimension for enhancing the quality of work life within the organization.

Providing employees the opportunity to become active participants and contributors to the overall success of the organization can foster a commitment to achieving the goals of the organization by making the goals of the organization the goals of the employee. McGregor's (1960) Theory Y presented the principle that employees are self-motivated and self-actualizing by their very nature and the effective leader will arrange the work environment to capitalize on those internal motivations to assist the employees in accomplishing the organizational goals.

Fear of change, maintenance of the status quo, and failure to provide participative opportunities for employees can create emotional conflict within the organization with resulting negative consequences. Argyris (1964) established an ongoing conflict between the individual and organization. He indicated organizational leaders can significantly impact the achievement of organizational goals when they provide viable opportunities for employees to contribute directly toward the organizational objectives and are recognized for those contributions. Argyris (1984) explained how organizations overemphasize the rational perspective of dealing with "just the facts" and minimize the impact of emotions, particularly negative emotions, in acquiring organizational goals.

Organizational researchers and leaders began to consider the effect emotions may have upon employees in the 1960s. Care and concern for people became a new approach for measuring the effectiveness of managers in addition to being concerned about the productivity of the employees. Blake and Mouton (1964) developed a managerial grid which illustrated the relationship between a manager's concern for production and concern for people. They also formulated a theory that suggested a leader who scored high on both concern for production and concern for people was the most effective organizational leader types. Likert (1967) suggested the need for leaders to concentrate on the values, expectations, and interpersonal skill competencies of their subordinates and peers. According to Likert, the positive leader is the one who builds self-esteem in others by demonstrating an appreciation of their work.

Not all theories addressed the issues of concern for people in all situations. Fiedler (1967) contended in his Leadership Contingency Model that 1) effective leadership is situational in nature requiring the leader to choose the most appropriate leadership behavior based upon the variables presented, 2) directive leaders are more effective in certain situations, and 3) leaders should be placed in situations where they may capitalize on their strengths. This model did not discount the aspect of empathy, caring, and concern but rather emphasized that leaders needed to be capable of responding appropriately whatever the situation. Emotionally intelligent leaders are capable of taking the most appropriate action, even as directive leaders when necessity requires, without losing sight of the need to empathetically consider subordinates and others when difficult circumstances arise (Ashkanasy & Dasborough, 2003; Barling, Slater, & Kelloway, 2000; Bar-On, Brown, Kirkcaldy, & Thomé, 2000; Carmeli, 2003; George, 2001; Malek, 2000; Sivanathan & Fekken, 2002; Stubbs, 2005; Wong & Law, 2002).

According to two theorists, leaders needed to concentrate on removing barriers that limited employees' opportunities to achieve organizational goals and providing employees' opportunities to participate in the decision-making process of the organization. House (1971) formulated the Path-Goal Model which suggested that the effective leader will increase the benefits to employees for achieving specific work goals. The effective leader accomplished the presentation of these benefits by reducing impediments which precluded the employees from attaining these goals. Vroom and Yetton's (1973) Decision-Making Model provided organizational leaders the opportunity to determine the amount of subordinate participation in decision-making. Effective leaders demonstrated the importance of subordinate decision-making by accepting and implementing the decision choices created by the employees in these circumstances.

In the latter part of the 20th century, theorists began to discuss the development, actualization, and value of employees within the organization. Leaders who could maximize the potential of their employees from a personal and professional perspective were providing a key component to the overall success of the organization. Blanchard and Hersey (1977) created the concept of Situational Leadership. This approach matched the leadership style of the leader to the developmental level and ability of the employee. This model also demonstrated a concern for employee development as well. Leadership flexibility afforded a greater effectiveness and appropriateness in one-on-one situations according to this model. Ouchi (1981) presented a set of seven principles that inculcated the values of cooperation, group support, loyalty, a sense of family closeness, and caring into the organization's leaders and employees. This approach removed the individualized pressure to perform and replaced it with a sense of value and accomplishment based upon the organization's overall accomplishments. Alderson (1985) introduced Theory R which presented a unique set of assumptions for leadership. The seven guiding suppositions developed a foundational principle: Everyone in the entire organization desired to be valued.

The concept of transforming leadership, particularly from the perspective of police leadership, was presented by Anderson (2000) as a viable option of leadership theory and practice in the 21st century. He defines it as follows:

> Transforming Leadership is vision, planning, communication, and creative action that have a positive unifying effect on a group of people around a set of clear values and beliefs, to accomplish a clear set of measurable goals. This transforming approach simultaneously impacts the personal development and corporate productivity of all involved (p. 307).

In order to create the necessary change within an organization, the transformational leader is in a constant state of refining and improving his or her approach to completing the goals. Anderson (2000) contended that the transforming leader is in a continual process of improving and developing, therein becoming a better leader or "an active agent of positive change" (p. 307). This assertion or belief extended to the idea that every police officer is a leader within his or her squad, division, department, and community.

All of the abovementioned theories, models, or philosophies present a unique conjecture for the consideration of emotional intelligence as an integral component in police leadership theories. Based upon these theories, we can assimilate a connection between one or more of the following emotional competencies or components (see Table 1) presented by Bar-On (1997, 2000).

Table 3

EQ-i Five Composite Scales and Fifteen Subscales

Intrapersonal Scales

      Emotional Self-Awareness, Assertiveness, Self-Regard, Self-Actualization, Independence

Interpersonal Scale

      Interpersonal Relationship, Social Responsibility, Empathy

Adaptability

      Problem Solving, Reality Testing, Flexibility

Stress Management

      Stress Tolerance, Impulse Control

General Mood

      Happiness, Optimism

Note: Adopted from Bar-On (1997a, 2000).

      Bar-On provided a description of the fifteen subscales represented in the previous table (see Appendix A). Based upon these descriptions, it appears that many of the emotional quotient subscales are reflected in the theories provided in this literature review. Many of the same terms used in the description of the theories are expressed in the descriptions of the emotional quotient subscales. In particular, the subscales of empathy, social responsibility, and interpersonal relationship echo the characteristics of leadership theories espoused by Westberg (1931), McGregor (1960), Bennis (1961), Blake and Mouton (1964), Arygris (1964), Likert (1967), Ouchi (1981), Alderson (1985), and Anderson (2000). The subscale of flexibility is expressed in Blanchard and Hersey's (1977) concept of situational leadership. Although undefined in the earlier theoretical constructs of leadership, emotional intelligence appeared to be an integral part of those theories.

Applying Emotional Intelligence to Law Enforcement Supervision

The concept of leadership appears to be infused throughout the entire law enforcement profession (Anderson, 2000). Encompassing everyone from the chief executive administrator to the "rookie" patrol officer, law enforcement agencies engender a responsibility of leadership either within the organization or within the community as a whole. Patrol officers are required to serve as community role models while police supervisors and administrators provide affirmative guidance and direction for their respective subordinates and the entire police organization.

The expectations may far exceed reality within many law enforcement organizations. Front line officers commit acts of violence against the citizens they are sworn to serve and protect while chief executive officers administer their agencies with the same draconian methods used by Marine Corps drill instructors during the 1960's.

Do police supervisors, with highly developed levels of emotional intelligence, have the capacity to effectively express themselves and listen more empathically to others in emotionally-charged and highly volatile circumstances? Bagshaw (2000) developed a framework for emotional intelligence that he identified by the acronym of CARES.

Table 4

CARES Framework of Emotional Intelligence

Creative tension

Active choice

Resilience under pressure

Empathic relationships

Self-awareness and self-control

Note. Adopted from Bagshaw, 2000, p. 63.

Currently, there are numerous studies that have been conducted regarding emotional intelligence within organizations and the potential effect or lack of effect of emotional intelligence on the organizational leadership (Barling, Slater, & Kelloway, 2000; Buford, 2001; Gardner & Stough, 2001; Higgs & Aitken, 2003; Langley, 2000; Malek, 2000; Palmer, Walls, Burgess, & Stough, 2000; Weinberger, 2003; Wong & Law, 2002) as well as books written on the subject (Caruso & Salovey, 2004; Cherniss & Adler, 2000; Cherniss & Goleman, 2001; Goleman, 1998).

In the current literature, only two studies (Bar-On, Brown, Kirkcaldy, & Thomé, 2000; Ricca, 2003) were found that have specifically involved police officers or police agencies and emotional intelligence. Bar-On, Brown, Kirkcaldy, and Thomé (2000) examined three groups of helping professionals relative to emotional intelligence. These three groups included police officers, educators working in the mental health profession, and child care workers.

Bar-On and his colleagues considered the adaptation relative to the occupational stress levels and the emotional intelligence of professionals in these occupational environments. Police officers scored significantly higher than either the child care workers or educators in terms of positive affect and emotional stability. Based upon these results, the researchers considered police officers as being better able to cope with stressful situations, more adaptable in general, and more aware of themselves and others than their counterparts in the other two helping professions (Bar-On, Brown, Kirkcaldy, & Thomé, 2000).

Ricca (2003) presented findings in her study indicating that the more competent police officers are in being aware of, understanding, and managing their emotions, the less frequently they experienced job burnout. Regression analysis supported the hypothesis that higher levels of emotional intelligence are associated with the enhanced belief in one's ability to successfully alleviate negative moods.

Culture, Stress, and Emotional Intelligence

Based upon information derived from this literature review, it appears that groups of people in either social or work environments adapt their behavior to the constraints, rules, and values constructed within that group's culture. The impact that the group culture brings to bear on its members is tremendously evident in the policing profession. Pogrebin and Poole (1991) expanded the notion that police culture socializes the police officer to repress his or her emotions in order to maintain a professional image in the eyes of the public, the department, and his or her peers. They indicated that an officer's authority and effectiveness would be severely compromised if the officer was unable to maintain "a poised presence even under the most tragic of circumstances" (p.397). In maintaining this professional shell of calm and stoic control, police officers impair their ability to experience the normal range of emotions that individuals are expected to exhibit during tragic events (Pogrebin & Poole, 1991; Stephens, Long, & Miller, 1997).

As an occupational hazard and an ingrained cultural standard, stress is a significant factor in the life of a law enforcement officer and the law enforcement supervisor. According to Brown and Campbell (1990), police sergeants experienced a greater amount of work overload and also reported more perceived stress than patrol officers; although according to Savery, Soutar, and Weaver (1993) and Lord (1996) police officers suffer significantly in silence to the pressures of stress. Given the parameters of police occupational stress, it would appear that emotional intelligence could potentially play a significant role in managing stress for individual officers and would be of potential benefit to the police organization as well (Crank & Caldero, 1991; Evans, Coman, & Stanley, 1992; Lord, 1996; Patterson, 2003; Stephens, Long, & Miller, 1997).

Within the construct of emotional intelligence, the ability to cope with stress is one measure of an individual's emotional intelligence. According to Bar-On (1997, 2000), stress tolerance (ST) is defined as the ability to withstand adverse events, stressful situations, and strong emotions without "falling apart." Persons who actively and positively cope with stress demonstrate a significant element of one's emotional intelligence competencies. It would appear that police officers may have adopted coping mechanisms that they employ to deal with the stressors of their specific occupation; however, they may not be appropriately dealing with their emotions from an intrapersonal perspective. This conjecture may also aid in the explanation of Bar-On,

Brown, Kirkcaldy and Thomé's (2000) study which indicated police officers scored higher on the EQ-i than other helping professionals in the area of stress management and tolerance.

One of the unfortunate consequences of prolonged stress can be job burnout within the police ranks. Emotional intelligence may possibly be a mitigating factor regarding stress and job burnout. Ricca (2003) examined the emotional intelligence levels and social competencies of police officers in order to predict job burnout for police. Regression analysis supported her main hypothesis which predicted an inverse relationship between emotional intelligence and job burnout.

Although other studies have not specifically addressed the issue of emotional intelligence and law enforcement officers directly, the lessons learned may have a direct bearing upon the impact of emotional intelligence to the law enforcement profession. Zacker and Bard (1973) discussed the implementation of programs designed to improve a police officer's capability to manage social and interpersonal conflict. Almost three decades prior to the coining of the term emotional intelligence, participants in one field study came from police officers assigned to the New York City Housing Authority. Training procedures for this group included group discussions, real-life simulations of interpersonal conflicts, role playing, and lectures which were all designed to improve the participants' ability to manage interpersonal conflicts by providing learning experiences that promoted active involvement by each participant. A controlled comparison of program participants found that for each criterion, program participants received the highest rank, denoting greatest improvement (or least decrement) on all ten performance measures (Zacker & Baird, 1973).

During the 1960s, social scientists also began to recognize the extent to which police are involved in interpersonal conflicts. Cherniss and Adler (2000) indicated that many police injuries occur when they intervene in interpersonal conflicts between individuals who know one another. Also, as mental institutions began to discharge their patients in large numbers (a trend referred to as "deinstitutionalization"), police were called upon more than ever to deal with complex psychological problems. In addition, changes in many inner-city communities put heavy strains on police-community relations and many people believed that lack of skill in managing interpersonal conflict on the part of the police either caused or exacerbated such strain.

All of these trends brought about an initiative to teach police how to resolve interpersonal conflict more effectively. Initially, such efforts met with considerable resistance from tradition-bound police departments steeped in a quasi-military culture. However, they gradually gained acceptance and today it would be difficult to find a large urban police department that has not used such training.

Although the world of academia at the professional graduate level may be a far stretch from the world of street-level law enforcement, the application of emotional intelligence may provide similar enhancements to both arenas. Jaeger (2001) advocated the implementation of emotional intelligence instruction and application to professional education courses in order to enhance academic performance at the graduate level and therein improve the interpersonal skills of those graduates in the workplace. Her study quantitatively illustrated that emotional intelligence was moderately correlated with academic performance; however, the qualitative data collected suggested that the emotional intelligence information acquired benefited the graduate students substantially on a personal level and may contribute to a better team player in the workplace.

The implications from Jaeger's (2001) study suggested a relationship between the emotional intelligence level espoused in one classroom and not espoused or expressed in another having a significant impact and increase in the students' emotional intelligence levels of those classes. This could possibly translate to a similar relationship between the emotional intelligence levels of line sergeants and the emotional intelligence levels of the officers that they supervise. Given that a higher level of emotional intelligence expressed by one sergeant will translate to an increase in the emotional intelligence level of his or her subordinates than that of a sergeant with a lower level of emotional intelligence on his or her subordinates, the implications for comparing the results of Jaeger's (2001) study to the research initiated by this investigator may yield favorable consequences.

CHAPTER 3

METHODOLOGY

The purpose of this study was to investigate the relationship between a patrol supervisor's level of emotional intelligence and that of his or her subordinate officers. This chapter will outline how the study was designed and implemented.

Research Design

The study employed a correlational research design in order to discover the relationship between a sergeant's emotional intelligence level (independent variable) and the emotional intelligence levels of the officers (dependent variable) that they supervise.

Participants

This study was conducted with the assistance of a law enforcement agency in the Southeastern United States. Tentative approval was acquired after meeting with the commanding officer of the agency in August 2004. The population initially consisted of 186 patrol sergeants and the 1,810 patrol officers directly under their commands.

The sample for this study was initially derived by randomly selecting 25 patrol sergeants and then purposely selecting the 148 respective patrol officers that they supervised from the population. Participation was to be entirely voluntary on the part of the sergeants and patrol officers. Any of the participants could withdraw at any time for any reason without organizational approval or threat of departmental censure.

Upon implementing the data collection phase for a period of three months, a grand total of 17 sergeants and 14 officers elected to participate. Numerous attempts were made to garner greater participation; however, the attempts failed to generate sufficient participation on the part of the randomly selected group of officers. An analysis of the data collected revealed that greater participation had occurred in geographic areas where the participants knew the researcher. Although randomization was compromised, it was determined that a convenience sample within the specified geographic area where the researcher was known to both the sergeants and officers would conceivably provide viable research data to this project.

The new convenience sample consisted of 23 sergeants and 153 officers. Data collection resumed and a grand total of 22 (96%) sergeants and 82 (54%) officers elected to participate. Although a smaller percentage of officers participated than was desired, the overall numbers were sufficient to proceed with the study.

Instruments

There were two instruments used in this study. The first instrument described is Bar-On's Emotional Quotient Inventory (EQ-i). According to Bar-On (2000), the EQ-i consists of 133 brief items and employs a five-point Likert scale ranging from 'very seldom true of me or not true of me' to 'very often true of me or true of me.' The reading level in English has been assessed at the North American sixth grade level. The EQ-i is suitable for administration to individuals seventeen years of age or older. The inventory takes approximately forty minutes to complete. Is should be noted that the online version of Bar-On's Emotional Quotient Inventory: 125 (EQ-i: 125) was used for the purpose of this study. This particular version of EQ-i consisted of 125 items. Eight questions were eliminated from this version that were not considered appropriate for hiring or employee selection purposes in some states. The questions dealt primarily with Negative Impression scale items such as "I feel cut off from my body" or "I think I've lost my mind" (Bar-On, 1997a, p. 6). It was determined that this version of the EQ-i psychometric properties should closely match those of the standard EQ-i and would, therefore, be more appropriate for this particular research study.

The EQ-i provides a total emotional quotient score and five composite scale scores that have 15 subscale scores. These five emotional quotient composite scales include 1) Intrapersonal, 2) Interpersonal, 3) Stress Management, 4) Adaptability, and 5) General Mood scores (Bar-On, 2000). The 15 subscales have been defined and are available for review (see Appendix A).

Normative values are based on the EQ-i scores of nearly 4,000 people worldwide. Test results are presented in standardized scores with a mean of 100 and a standard deviation of 15. Higher EQ-i scores indicate a higher level of emotional intelligence (Bar-On, 1997). The EQ-i is currently the most extensively used and researched test of emotional intelligence. It has demonstrated good reliability with an average internal consistency of .76 and average retest reliability of .85 after one month. The validity of the EQ-i has been well established. In terms of predictive validity, which is relevant to this study, the EQ-i has shown to predict occupational success in a sample of Air Force recruiters (Bar-On, 1997). Brackett and Mayer (2004) indicated published reliability coefficients (Cronbach Alpha values), estimating internal consistency, for Bar-On's EQ-i across the 15 subscales that comprise these factor scores with a range of .69 to .86 relevant to ten studies.

Bar-On (1997) has established an effective scoring process for the EQ-i that is useful in making statistical comparisons among and between groups which will be very critical in this study.

EQ-i raw scores are converted to standard scores based on a mean of "100" and a standard deviation of 15 (similar to IQ scores). EQ-i raw scores are of limited value on their own. Converting EQ-i raw scores to standard scores facilitates comparisons of a respondent's scores to the scores of the normative group and theoretically, the rest of the population. Higher EQ-i scores (above 100) indicate "emotional intelligent" people [having enhanced emotional intelligence skills], while lower scores indicate a need to improve "emotional skills" in specific areas [emotional skills need improvement]. This scoring structure is similar to the IQ scoring structure, which renders a Full IQ that is divided into a Verbal IQ and a Performance IQ, based on subscale scores that describe aspects of cognitive intelligence – hence, the term "EQ" (Emotional Quotient) was coined by the author [Bar-On] in 1985 to describe this parallel approach (Bar-On, 1997b, p. 8).

Bar-On (1997a) established that the EQ-i has a normal distribution of values which have been demonstrated based upon the extensive research conducted by both the author and further explored by the publisher of the instrument.

The majority of respondents (approximately 68%) will receive scores within 15 points of the mean (i.e. between 85 and 115). An even larger majority (about 95%) will be within 30 points of the mean (i.e. between 70 and 130, and virtually all respondents (approximately 99%) will receive scores within 45 points of the mean (i.e. between 55 and 145). Respondents whose overall scores are under 70 and over 130 are markedly atypical and need to be examined more closely (Bar-On, 1997a, 39).

Table 5 illustrates the standards for interpreting EQ-i scores as represented in the

Emotional Quotient Inventory (EQ-i) Technical Manual (Bar-On, 1997a). Sergeant and

officer scores in this study ranged from 68 to 131. A score below 70 indicates atypical

impaired emotional capacity; whereas, a score of more than 130 indicates an atypically

well developed emotional capacity.

Table 5

Interpretative Guidelines for EQ-I Scores

Standard	Interpretative Guidelines
130+	Markedly High – atypically well-developed emotional capacity
120-129	Very High – extremely well developed emotional capacity
110-119	High – well developed emotional capacity
90-109	Average – adequate emotional capacity
80-89	Low – underdeveloped emotional capacity, requiring improvement
70-79	Very Low – extremely underdeveloped emotional capacity requiring Improvement
Under 70	Markedly low – atypically impaired emotional capacity, requiring improvement

Note. Adopted from Bar-On, 1997a, p. 40.

The Bar-On's EQ-i was supplemented with the use of a questionnaire to obtain

demographic information. This questionnaire, developed by the researcher, attempted to

capture the participant's years of employment with the agency, total years of experience

in law enforcement, assignment area (rural or urban), educational levels or credentials,

rank (e.g., sergeant, patrol officer), years of supervisory experience with the agency

(sergeant) or years of patrol experience with the agency (officer), prior years of law enforcement supervisory experience (sergeant) or prior law enforcement experience with other agencies (officer), the respondent's assessment of their perceived emotional intelligence level, and the respondent's assessment of either his or her subordinates' perceived emotional intelligence level or his or her supervisor's perceived emotional intelligence level. This questionnaire was used to distinguish differences and test for significance within and between specific groups.

Procedures

The researcher submitted to North Carolina State University's Institutional Review Board for the Protection of Human Subjects in Research (IRB) a request for approval of this study. The approval for this research study was acquired from the IRB on June 30, 2005.

Written permission from the commander of the law enforcement agency was obtained on July 7, 2005 to proceed with the implementation of this study and indicating an organizational approval and support of this study. Informed consent forms for research were prepared for each participant to acknowledge participation in the research project prior to accessing the test instruments.

A total of 25 sergeants were initially randomly selected from the population for testing purposes within this study. Each participating sergeant received 1) a letter of invitation to participate in the study, 2) a Consent to Participate document that outlines the purpose of the study and the rules governing the conduct of the researcher, and 3) an informed consent form that they could read and print for their personal records prior to taking the EQ-i. Upon agreeing to participate in this study, the respondent submitted an email to the researcher indicating his or her desire to take part in the study. The researcher, upon receipt of the sergeant's email, submitted an acknowledgment email to the respondent detailing the online location of the EQ-i and demographic profile questionnaire as well as assigning the respondent a unique identifier for purposes of confidentiality. The EQ-i and demographic profile questionnaire delivered electronic to the sergeants in July - August, 2005. Results of each sergeant's individual EQ-i scores were assimilated and returned to them with an explanation of the results.

All of the patrol officers who are supervised by the selected sergeants were purposely selected to receive the EQ-i. Each selected officer received 1) a letter of invitation to participate in the study, 2) a Consent to Participate document that outlines the purpose of the study and the rules governing the conduct of the researcher, and 3) an informed consent form that they may read and print for their personal records prior to taking the EQ-i. Upon agreeing to participate in this study, the respondent was to submit an email to the researcher indicating his or her desire to be a part of the study. The researcher would then submit an email to the respondent detailing the online location of the EQ-i and demographic profile questionnaire as well as assigning the respondent a unique identifier for purposes of confidentiality. The EQ-i and demographic profile questionnaire were to be delivered electronically to the patrol officers in August, 2005. Results of the patrol officers' individual EQ-i scores were to be assimilated and returned to them with an explanation of the results.

As previously indicated the random selection of participants did not materialize over a period of three months. A revised process was instituted in a geographic area where the sergeants and officers knew the researcher personally. The revised process was exactly the same for the convenience sample of sergeants as it had been for the random selection of sergeants; however, a significant change was implemented for the collection of data from the officers supervised by the new sample of sergeants.

Revisions to the procedures for data collection of officers consisted of using a pen and paper version of Bar-On's EQ-i as well as a pen and paper copy of the Officer's Demographic Profile. The test material was disseminated throughout the selected geographic region with specific instructions as to the administration of the exam and completion of the demographic profile. Administrative staff assisted in administering the exam to the officers at various times during a three-week timeframe. The researcher collected the completed tests and profiles during the last week of October 2005.

The researcher manually entered the responses into the online version of Bar-On's EQ-i and acquired immediate feedback of the results. The officers' results were printed, placed in a sealed envelope, and delivered to the respective division offices along with a feedback letter and explanation of the results.

Data Analysis

Descriptive statistics were computed for each group and subgroup within the study using SPSS-12.0. Pearson product-moment correlation analysis was used to determine if a linear correlation exists between the EQ-i score of a patrol sergeant and the EQ-i scores of the patrol officers under his or her supervision. Additionally, a t-test was conducted to determine differences between the mean scores of sergeants and their respective officers.

CHAPTER 4

FINDINGS

Overview of the Study

The purpose of this study was to investigate the relationship between a patrol supervisor's level of emotional intelligence and that of his or her subordinate officers. Data were collected from a convenience sample of 22 patrol sergeants and 82 patrol officers supervised by these sergeants from a law enforcement agency in the Southeastern United States. The independent variables were the sergeants' Total Emotional Quotient Inventory (EQ-i) score and five Composite Scale scores of Intrapersonal EQ, Interpersonal EQ, Stress Management EQ, Adaptability EQ, and General Mood EQ. The dependent variables were the patrol officers' mean Total EQ-i score and five mean Composite Scale scores of Intrapersonal EQ, Interpersonal EQ, Stress Management EQ, Adaptability EQ, and General Mood EQ supervised by their respective sergeant. The independent variables were regressed with the dependent variables in order to investigate the relationship between a patrol supervisor's level of emotional intelligence and their respective patrol officers' emotional intelligence levels. This chapter presents an overview of the study, the results of the data analyses, findings of the study based on the research question, and a summary of the findings.

The Target Population

Based upon the most recent crime statistics compiled by the Federal Bureau of Investigation (FBI), the total number of sworn law enforcement officers in the United States, as of October 31, 2002, was 428,365. Within eleven southeastern states, the ranks of sworn law enforcement officers consisted of 162,800 sworn officers (FBI, 2005). Of this total, 143,340 (88%) sworn law enforcement officers were male and 19,460 (12%) were female.

The target population indicated for this study was drawn from a law enforcement agency in the Southeastern United States consisting of 186 line sergeants and 1,810 patrol officers under the command of the line sergeants. Initially, a random sample of 25 line sergeants was selected along with the 148 respective patrol officers under their command.

Upon implementing the data collection phase for a period of three months, a grand total of 17 sergeants and 14 officers elected to participate. Numerous attempts were made to garner greater participation. Direct telephone contact was made with several sergeants requesting their assistance in encouraging their officers to participate. Three emails were sent to all sergeants requesting their assistance in encouraging their officers to participate. Command personnel were contacted directly in regards to making an appeal to all officers involved in the study to encourage them to participate. However, none of these additional measures, implemented over a period of two months, were successful in increasing the response rate. An analysis of the data collected revealed that greater participation had occurred in geographic areas where the participants knew the researcher. Although randomization was compromised, it was determined that a convenience sample within the specified geographic area where the researcher was known to both the sergeants and officers would conceivably provide viable research data to this project.

Based upon the difficulty in collecting data among the patrol officers of randomly selected sergeants, a change ensued that allowed for the collection of data from a convenience sample of 23 sergeants and 153 patrol officers under their command. At the conclusion of the data collection process, 22 (96%) line sergeants and 82 (54%) patrol officers participated in this study.

Although the original random selection of sergeants and their respective officers was abandoned in an effort to acquire a complete data set, 17 sergeants of the original 25 participated to a limited degree. Limited data were gathered that provided a view of the homogeneity of the random sample as compared to the convenience sample. Table 6 provides an illustration of the homogeneity of both groups. Significant similarities exists between the two groups regarding age, sex, total years working at the rank of sergeant, total number years supervising their current officers, and total number of years working with the current police agency.

Table 6

Homogeneity of Randomly Selected Sergeants and Convenience Sample Sergeants

Characteristics	Randomly Selected	Convenience
Mean age	40.2	41
Sex		
Male	16	21
Female	1	1
Total mean years as sergeant	3.27 [a]	3.65 [b]
Total mean years supervising current officers	2.5 [a]	3.55 [b]
Total mean years working with police agency	15.27 [a]	11.66 [b]
Assigned geographic patrol area		
Small Rural County	2	11
Medium Rural County	4	4
Large County	3	5
Metropolitan Area	3	0
Educational credentials		
High school diploma / GED	0	5
Some college	4	6
Associate's degree	2	4
Bachelor's degree	6	5
Mean total EQ-i score	102.0588235	107.2380952
Standard deviation of mean total EQ-i scores	10.67983256	12.77460278

Note. Randomly selected sample n = 17. Convenience sample n = 22.
[a] Five participants did not complete the demographic profile for this study.
[b] Two participants did not complete the demographic profile for this study.

Similarities existed in the geographic assignment areas regarding rural, medium population counties (populations greater than 50,000 but less than 100,000) and large population counties (populations greater than 100,000); whereas a contrast occurred within the rural, small counties (populations under 50,000) depicting the convenience sample as having more than fifty percent selecting this geographic grouping and the random sample having none designating this grouping. Additionally, the random sample designated three participants being assigned to metropolitan city environments and the convenience sample having none in this geographic assignment area.

Similarities also existed in the area of educational credentials. Both samples indicated very similar numbers represented by the variables of "some college," "associate's degree," and "bachelor's degree" credentialed sergeants with a contrast occurring only in the variable of "high school diploma /GED" credentialed sergeants. In the convenience sample, twenty percent of the sergeants indicated having a "high school diploma /GED" as their highest level of academic achievement; whereas, in the random sample no sergeants indicated this being their highest level of academic achievement.

Two other areas of similarity that should be noted between the two groups are the mean total EQ-i scores and the standard deviation of the mean total EQ-i scores. There exists only a five-point differential in the mean total EQ-i score of the convenience sample as compared to the randomly selected sample. There also exists only a two-point differential in the standard deviation of the mean total EQ-i scores of the convenience sample as compared to the randomly selected sample.

Although significant data are missing regarding the officers supervised by the sergeants of the randomly selected sample, the researcher is confident that the findings would have been similar to the convenience sample had data been collected and analyzed on the randomly selected group.

The convenience sample of sergeants is demographically described and illustrated in Table 7. This table conveys the demographic characteristic of the sergeants participating in the study in conjunction with the sample size (n) and either the appropriate mean score or percentage for the specific characteristic described.

Table 7

Descriptive Statistics of Line Sergeants Participating in Study

Characteristic	n	M	P
Age	22	41	
Sex	22		
Male	21		96%
Female	1		4%
Total years as sergeant	20[a]	3.65	
Total years supervising current officers	20[a]	3.55	
Total years working with police agency	20[a]	11.66	
Assigned geographic patrol area	20[a]		
Small Rural County	11		50%
Medium Rural County	4		18.2%
Large County	5		22.7%
Educational credentials	20[a]		
High school diploma / GED	5		22.7%
Some college	6		27.3%
Associate's degree	4		18.2%
Bachelor's degree	5		22.7%

Note. n = 22.

[a] Two participants did not complete the demographic profile for this study.

The convenience sample of patrol officers is described demographically and illustrated in Table 8. This table conveys the demographic characteristic of the patrol officers participating in the study in conjunction with the sample size (n) and either the appropriate mean score or percentage for the specific characteristic described.

Table 8

Descriptive Statistics of Patrol Officers Participating in Study

Characteristic	n	M	P
Age	82	36.5	
Sex	82		
Male	78		95.1%
Female	4		4.9%
Total years as officer	76[a]	10.28	
Total years working with police agency	76[a]	10.15	
Total years supervising current officers	76[a]	3.45	
Assigned geographic patrol area	76[a]		
Small Rural County	47		57.3%
Medium Rural County	18		21.9%
Large County	11		13.4%
Educational credentials	76[a]		
High school diploma / GED	15		18.3%
Some college	25		30.5%
Associate's degree	19		23.2%
Bachelor's degree	17		20.7%

Note. n = 82.

[a] Six participants did not complete the demographic profile for this study.

Statistical Analysis

Descriptive Statistics

Descriptive statistics (Table 9) explained the means and standard deviations of the data collected through the EQ-i for both line sergeants and the respective patrol officers that they supervise. As demonstrated by the mean (M) total EQ-i and Composite EQ-i scores, sergeants scored approximately six points higher than did the officers that they supervised.

Table 9

Means and Standard Deviations for the Study Variables

Variable	N	M	Range	SD
Sergeants' Total EQ-i score	22	107.24	76 – 131	12.77
Sergeants' Composite EQ-i scores				
Intrapersonal	22	107.86	70 – 130	14.20
Interpersonal	22	101.29	80 – 118	10.62
Adaptability	22	108.67	89 – 132	11.09
Stress Management	22	106.86	85 – 135	13.06
General Mood	22	105.33	72 – 122	11.80
Officers' Total EQ-i score	82	100.26	68 – 129	13.39
Officers' Composite EQ-i scores				
Intrapersonal	82	101	71 – 130	12.66
Interpersonal	82	96.59	68 – 128	13.43
Adaptability	82	104.46	79 – 131	13.43
Stress Management	82	100.37	71 – 128	13.55
General Mood	82	100.28	62 – 127	13.71

Correlational Analysis

Data were collected from the convenience sample of sergeants (n = 22) and officers (n = 82) within the respective squads that they supervised. A comprehensive correlation matrix was developed (Table 10) using Pearson product-moment correlation analysis. Table 10 demonstrates the correlations between the test results of the sergeants and the mean test results of the squad of officers supervised by each respective sergeant.

Table 10

Intercorrelations among Patrol Sergeants' Total EQ-i and Composite Scale Scores and Patrol Officers'
Mean Total EQ-i and Composite Scale Scores

Variables						Variables (Composite Scales)						
(Composite Scales)	A	B	C	D	E	F	G	H	I	J	K	L
A. Sergeants' EQ-i Total Scores												
B. Sergeants' Intrapersonal Scores	.943**											
C. Sergeants' Interpersonal Scores	.754**	.682**										
D. Sergeants' Stress Management Scores	.765**	.613**	.353									
E. Sergeants' Adaptability Scores	.890**	.763**	.551**	.845**								
F. Sergeants' General Mood Scores	.927**	.857**	.783**	.646*	.760**							
G. Officers' Mean EQ-i Total Scores	.038	.054	-.040	-.045	.075	.079						
H. Officers' Mean Intrapersonal Scores	.118	.070	-.021	.156	.180	.096	.840**					
I. Officers' Mean Interpersonal Scores	-.173	-.066	-.305	-.323	-.144	-.083	.622**	.254				
J. Officers' Mean Stress Management Scores	.089	.085	.114	.024	.062	.170	.798**	.486*	.466*			
K. Officers' Mean Adaptability Scores	.049	.052	.029	-.031	.061	.114	.942**	.736**	.556*	.836**		
L. Officers' Mean General Mood Scores	.037	.066	.026	-.081	.075	.031	.939**	.807**	.495*	.712**	.857**	

**. Correlation is significant at the 0.01 level (2-tailed)

*. Correlation is significant at the 0.05 level (2-tailed)

The correlational analysis most germane to this study centered on the relationship between the Sergeants' EQ-i and Composite Scale Scores and the Officers' Mean EQ-i and Composite Scale Scores. No statistically significant correlations were demonstrated between these variables. Table 11 illustrates the results of correlational analysis addressing the Sergeants' EQ-i Total Scores and the study's dependent variables. There was no significant correlation found between the Sergeants' Total EQ-i and the Officers' Mean Total EQ-i, Mean Intrapersonal Composite Score, Mean Interpersonal Composite Score, Mean Stress Management Composite Score, or Mean General Mood Composite Score.

Table 11

Intercorrelations between Sergeants' Total EQ-i Scores and the Study Variables

Variable	N	r	p-value
Officers' Mean Total EQ-i Score	19[a]	.038	.877
Officers' Mean Intrapersonal Composite Score	19[a]	.118	.629
Officers' Mean Interpersonal Composite Score	19[a]	-.173	.478
Officers' Mean Stress Management Composite Score	19[a]	.089	.716
Officers' Mean Adaptability Composite Score	19[a]	.049	.842
Officers' Mean General Mood Composite Score	19[a]	.037	.882

[a] Nineteen squads were reported containing 82 subordinate patrol officers of the 22 sergeants participating in the study.

Table 12 illustrates the results of correlational analysis addressing the Sergeants'

Intrapersonal Composite Scores and the study's dependent variables. There was no

significant correlation found between the Sergeants' Intrapersonal Composite Scores and

the Officers' Mean Total EQ-i, Mean Intrapersonal Composite Score, Mean Interpersonal

Composite Score, Mean Stress Management Composite Score, or Mean General Mood

Composite Score.

Table 12

Intercorrelations between Sergeants' Intrapersonal Composite Scores

and the Study Variables

Variable	N	r	p-value
Officers' Mean Total EQ-i Score	19[a]	.054	.826
Officers' Mean Intrapersonal Composite Score	19[a]	.070	.774
Officers' Mean Interpersonal Composite Score	19[a]	-.066	.787
Officers' Mean Stress Management Composite Score	19[a]	.085	.728
Officers' Mean Adaptability Composite Score	19[a]	.052	.832
Officers' Mean General Mood Composite Score	19[a]	.066	.787

[a] Nineteen squads were reported containing 82 subordinate patrol officers of the 22
sergeants participating in the study.

Table 13 illustrates the results of correlational analysis addressing the Sergeants'

Interpersonal Composite Scores and the study's dependent variables. There was no

significant correlation found between the Sergeants' Interpersonal Composite Score and

the Officers' Mean Total EQ-i, Mean Intrapersonal Composite Score, Mean Interpersonal

Composite Score, Mean Stress Management Composite Score, or Mean General Mood

Composite Score.

Table 13

Intercorrelations between Sergeants' Interpersonal Composite Scores

and the Study Variables

Variable	N	r	p-value
Officers' Mean Total EQ-i Score	19[a]	-.040	.869
Officers' Mean Intrapersonal Composite Score	19[a]	-.021	.931
Officers' Mean Interpersonal Composite Score	19[a]	-.305	.204
Officers' Mean Stress Management Composite Score	19[a]	.114	.643
Officers' Mean Adaptability Composite Score	19[a]	.029	.907
Officers' Mean General Mood Composite Score	19[a]	.026	.916

[a] Nineteen squads were reported containing 82 subordinate patrol officers of the 22 sergeants participating in the study.

Table 14 illustrates the results of correlational analysis addressing the Sergeants'

Stress Management Composite Scores and the study's dependent variables. There was

no significant correlation found between the Sergeants' Stress Management Composite

Score and the Officers' Mean Total EQ-i, Mean Intrapersonal Composite Score, Mean

Interpersonal Composite Score, Mean Stress Management Composite Score, or Mean

General Mood Composite Score.

Table 14

Intercorrelations between Sergeants' Stress Management Composite Scores

and the Study Variables

Variable	N	r	p-value
Officers' Mean Total EQ-i Score	19[a]	.045	.855
Officers' Mean Intrapersonal Composite Score	19[a]	.156	.525
Officers' Mean Interpersonal Composite Score	19[a]	-.323	.177
Officers' Mean Stress Management Composite Score	19[a]	.024	.924
Officers' Mean Adaptability Composite Score	19[a]	-.031	.899
Officers' Mean General Mood Composite Score	19[a]	-.081	.743

[a] Nineteen squads were reported containing 82 subordinate patrol officers of the 22 sergeants participating in the study.

Table 15 illustrates the results of correlational analysis addressing the Sergeants' Adaptability Composite Scores and the study's dependent variables. There was no significant correlation found between the Sergeants' Adaptability Composite Score and the Officers' Mean Total EQ-i, Mean Intrapersonal Composite Score, Mean Interpersonal Composite Score, Mean Stress Management Composite Score, or Mean General Mood Composite Score.

Table 15

Intercorrelations between Sergeants' Adaptability Composite Scores

and the Study Variables

Variable	N	r	p-value
Officers' Mean Total EQ-i Score	19[a]	.075	.761
Officers' Mean Intrapersonal Composite Score	19[a]	.180	.461
Officers' Mean Interpersonal Composite Score	19[a]	-.144	.558
Officers' Mean Stress Management Composite Score	19[a]	.062	.802
Officers' Mean Adaptability Composite Score	19[a]	.061	.804
Officers' Mean General Mood Composite Score	19[a]	.075	.759

[a] Nineteen squads were reported containing 82 subordinate patrol officers of the 22 sergeants participating in the study.

Table 16 illustrates the results of correlational analysis addressing the Sergeants' General Mood Composite Scores and the study's dependent variables. There was no significant correlation found between the Sergeants' General Mood Composite Scores and the Officers' Mean Total EQ-i, Mean Intrapersonal Composite Score, Mean Interpersonal Composite Score, Mean Stress Management Composite Score, or Mean General Mood Composite Score.

Table 16

Intercorrelations between Sergeants' General Mood Composite Scores

and the Study Variables

Variable	N	r	p-value
Officers' Mean Total EQ-i Score	19[a]	.079	.749
Officers' Mean Intrapersonal Composite Score	19[a]	.096	.696
Officers' Mean Interpersonal Composite Score	19[a]	-.083	.735
Officers' Mean Stress Management Composite Score	19[a]	.170	.487
Officers' Mean Adaptability Composite Score	19[a]	.114	.642
Officers' Mean General Mood Composite Score	19[a]	.031	.901

[a] Nineteen squads were reported containing 82 subordinate patrol officers of the 22 sergeants participating in the study.

Analysis of Mean Score Differences

An analysis of mean score differences between sergeants (n = 22) and officers (n = 82) regarding the study variables of Total EQ-i and the five composite subscales. As illustrated by Table 17, the mean score differences between the two groups produced no statistically significant values for any of the study variables. The variable Total EQ-i mean score for sergeants (M = 107.32) and officers (M = 100.21) produced a t-value of 2.24 and a p-value of .027. The variable Interpersonal Composite mean score for sergeants (M = 107.91) and officers (M = 99.89) produced a t-value of 2.19 and a p-value of .031. The variable Interpersonal Composite mean score for sergeants (M = 102.05) and officers (M = 96.41) produced a t-value of 1.80 and a p-value of .075. The variable

Stress Management Composite mean score for sergeants (M = 108.27) and officers (M = 104.38) produced a t-value of 1.25 and a p-value of .214. The variable Adaptability Composite mean score for sergeants (M = 106.68) and officers (M = 98.98) produced a t-value of 2.03 and a p-value of .045. The variable General Mood Composite mean score for sergeants (M = 105.73) and officers (M = 100.37) produced a t-value of 1.68 and a p-value of .096.

Table 17

Analysis of Mean Score Differences Between Sergeants and Patrol Officers on Study Variables

Variable	Groups		t-value	p-value
	Sergeants (N = 22)	Officers (N = 82)		
Total EQ-I Score	107.32	100.21	2.24	.027
Interpersonal Score	107.91	99.89	2.19	.031
Interpersonal Score	102.05	96.41	1.80	.075
Stress Management Score	108.27	104.38	1.25	.214
Adaptability Score	106.68	98.98	2.03	.045
General Mood Score	105.73	100.37	1.68	.096

Hypotheses Testing

Research Question One

Research Question One investigated if there was a relationship between the emotional intelligence level of the patrol supervisor and the emotional intelligence level of the subordinate patrol officer. The null hypothesis (H_{01}) states that there is not a statistically significant correlation between the emotional intelligence level of the patrol supervisor and the emotional intelligence level of the subordinate patrol officer. In the statistical analysis, the correlation coefficients between the Sergeants' Total EQ-i and five Composite Subscale Scores and the Officers' Total EQ-i and five Composite Subscale Scores never attained a statistically significant value within the entire analyses (see Tables 11, 12, 13, 14, 15, and 16). Therefore, the null hypothesis was retained.

Summary of the Findings

The data gathered from the convenience sample of 22 sergeants and 19 respective squads representing 82 subordinate patrol officers supervised by the sergeants were presented and analyzed based on the results of the Bar-On Emotional Quotient Inventory (EQ-i) scores. The data were presented in tables illustrating the bivariate relationships between the Sergeants' Total EQ-i and five Composite Subscale scores and the Officers' Mean Total EQ-i and five Composite Subscale scores. The bivariate correlational analyses were done using the Pearson Product-Moment Coefficient of Correlation (r) to determine the strength of the relationship among the Sergeants' Total EQ-i and five Composite Subscale scores and the Officers' Mean Total EQ-i and five Composite Subscale scores.

Additionally, an analysis of mean score differences (t-value) between the sergeants and patrol officers was conducted to investigate the significance of difference between the two populations when the population variances are unknown but equal. Based upon this analysis, no statistically significant relationships were determined between the sergeants and patrol officers.

As a result of the correlational analysis (r) for the dependent variables of Officers' Total EQ-i and five Composite Subscale scores as measured by the independent variables Sergeants' EQ-i and five Composite Subscale scores, the null of hypothesis one (H_{01}) was retained. There was not a statistically significant relationship between the study's independent and dependent variables.

CHAPTER 5

DISCUSSION

This research study was undertaken to investigate the relationship between the emotional intelligence of line sergeants and their subordinate patrol officers. Law enforcement officers, by virtue of the very nature of their jobs, find themselves frequently embroiled in highly stressful and emotionally charged situations. These volatile circumstances have the potential of becoming very dangerous for all persons involved. The capacity of a law enforcement officer to maintain control of his or her emotions, thereby assisting in the de-escalation of the stressful situation, could be considered a very valuable asset in all police personnel.

Recognizing and appreciating the impact that persons demonstrating high emotional intelligence can have in and on emotionally explosive conditions is an attribute most police agencies would desire in their personnel. Determining whether the emotional intelligence of a supervisor could potentially contribute to the emotional intelligence of a subordinate may perhaps be a significant concern to the law enforcement community.

Introduction

Supervisory personnel, more specifically line sergeants, provide the direction for as well as "view, monitor and interact with those who are performing the core functions of policing (Harrison, 2001, p. 151)." Researchers have determined that the front line supervisor of police officers can directly influence the attitudes and behavior of their subordinate personnel (Engel & Worden, 2003; Mastrofski, Parks, Reiss & Worden, 1999, 1998). Additionally, researchers and authors advancing the influence of emotional intelligence on leadership effectiveness are prolific (Ashkanasy & Dasborough, 2003; Barling, Slater, & Kelloway, 2000; Brooks, 2002; Carmeli, 2003; Cherniss & Adler,

2000; Cooper & Sawaf, 1997; Feldman, 1999; Gardner & Stough, 2002; George, 2000;

Goleman, 1998; Hartsfield, 2003; Langley, 2000; Johnson & Indvik, 1999; Massey,

1999; Møller & Powell, 2001; Palmer, Walls, Burgess, & Stough, 2001; Schulte, 2003;

Sivanathan & Fekken, 2002; Stubbs, 2005; Wong & Law, 2002).

If, in fact, police supervisory personnel have a direct influence on the attitudes and behavior of their subordinates and if emotional intelligence influences leadership effectiveness, then it should conceivably be prudent to speculate that the supervisor's emotional intelligence level would be linked to the emotional intelligence level of the subordinate officer.

The purpose of this exploratory study was to determine if a relationship existed between the line sergeant's emotional intelligence and the emotional intelligence of his or her subordinate officers. If such a correlation exists, the enhancement of the emotional intelligence level of the sergeant could potentially augment the emotional intelligence level of the subordinate officers under his or her supervision by providing a positive example for the subordinates to emulate. This emulation could thereby possibly translate to a higher level of emotional intelligence observed in the subordinate officer.

Overview of the Study, Research Question, and Hypothesis

Overview of the Study

The purpose of this study was to determine if a relationship existed between the emotional intelligence of a patrol sergeant and the emotional intelligence of the subordinate officers that he or she supervised. One primary research question was posed and data were collected in order to address the corresponding hypothesis.

Research Question One

Is there a significant correlation between the emotional intelligence of a patrol sergeant and the emotional intelligence of the subordinate officers that he or she supervises?

H_{01}: There is no statistically significant correlation between the emotional intelligence of a patrol sergeant and the subordinate officers that he or she supervises.

In the statistical analysis, the correlation coefficients between the Sergeants' Total EQ-i and five Composite Subscale Scores and the Officers' Total EQ-i and five Composite Subscale Scores were not statistically significant within the entire analyses (see Tables 11, 12, 13, 14, 15, and 16); therefore, the null hypothesis was retained.

The variable Total EQ-i mean score for sergeants was 107.32 and the Total EQ-i mean score for officers was 100.21. The variable Interpersonal Composite mean score for sergeants was 107.91 and the Interpersonal Composite mean score for officers was 99.89. The variable Interpersonal Composite mean score for sergeants was 102.05 and the Interpersonal Composite mean score for officers was 96.41. The variable Stress Management Composite mean score for sergeants was 108.27 and the Stress Management Composite mean score for officers was 104.38. The variable Adaptability Composite mean score for sergeants was 106.68 and the Adaptability Composite mean score for officers was 98.98. The variable General Mood Composite mean score for sergeants was 105.73 and the General Mood Composite mean score for officers was 100.37.

Although these variables are not statistically significant they nevertheless present an interesting phenomenon for discussion. There exists, within this study, approximately a five-point differential between the variables reported for the sergeants' EQ-i mean

scores and the mean EQ-i scores of the officers supervised by the sergeants. This

differential may be explained by the mean age of the sergeants (41) and the mean age of

the patrol officers (36.5) that are supervised by the sergeants. According to Bar-On

(1997a), the "age effects suggest that emotional intelligence increases with age and, thus

changes throughout life" (p.83). Bar-On (1997a) also established, in the norming of the

EQ-i, the following age groupings of 1) under age 20, 2) 20 – 29 years of age, 3) 30 – 39

years of age , 4) 40 – 49 years of age, and 5) 50 years of age or over. Bar-On (1997a,

p. 83 – 84) presented his ANOVA results for the age effect which indicated 40 – 49 years

of age to be the age grouping with the highest average EQ-i scores.

　　　In addition to age, other factors could potentially aid in the explanation of the

differences between sergeants and their subordinate officers. A multi-faceted factor that

may contribute to this difference between the sergeants and officers could possibly be the

life and career experiences each have encountered. It would be fair to assume that the

sergeants, as a whole, may exhibit a higher level of emotional intelligence simply by

having achieved the rank of sergeant. The fact that the sergeant would have to be capable

of managing subordinates and responding to his or her superior officers would indicate a

capacity to 1) appraise one's own emotions and express those emotions to others

effectively; 2) recognize emotional responses in others, empathetically gauge the proper

affective response, and choose the most socially adaptive behavior in response; 3)

regulate and enhance one's own mood and the moods of others thereby motivating others

toward the accomplishment of a particular goal or end; and 4) solve problems adaptively

by integrating emotional considerations when choosing alternatives to a particular

problem or issue (Salovey & Mayer, 1990).

The rank of sergeant is replete with circumstances of handling disgruntled subordinates, demanding superiors, and irate citizens. Being able to manage one's own emotional responses in these situations could potentially indicate a basis for exhibiting a higher level of emotional intelligence than the subordinate patrol officer. Additionally, the sergeant would have to deal with a plethora of stress-inducing circumstances beyond those faced by the patrol officer.

Issues such as: 1) handling office politics, 2) meeting official deadlines for the submission of required documents and projects, 3) managing budget constraints and shortfalls, 4) conducting performance appraisals, 5) resolving personnel grievances, 6) creating and managing work schedules, 7) adjusting work schedules due to personnel shortages, 8) handling disciplinary action of subordinates, 9) conducting internal investigations of personnel, 10) investigating and dealing with citizen complaints against patrol officers, 11) being held vicariously liable for subordinate personnel's actions, 12) dealing with civil litigation claims, 13) avoiding discrimination lawsuits; are among the many considerations that a sergeant may be called upon to deal with above and beyond the stressors of being a police officer. Managing the multitude of responsibilities incumbent upon the patrol supervisor may help explain differences between the supervisor's emotional intelligence and that of his or her subordinate patrol officers.

Consideration and reflection must be made regarding the lack of correlation between the variables of this study. Was the lack of correlation due to the test instrument used in the study? Bar-On's online Emotional Quotient Inventory (EQ-i 125) instrument, a self-report measure of emotional intelligence, was used in this study. It is worthy of consideration that the Bar-On EQ-360 could have been a better measure of the emotional intelligence of sergeants and their subordinate officer. The Bar-On EQ-360 is a

scientifically valid instrument with excellent scale and subscale reliability (MHS, 2006).
This instrument's primary goal is to provide a means of combining the external
impressions of a person's emotional intelligence with his or her own self-rating of
emotional intelligence. The capacity of this instrument to provide multiple perspectives
of an individual's emotional intelligence aids in the reduction of bias associated with a
self-reporting instrument. The instrument also allows for the recruitment of six rater
groups comprised of managers, peers, direct reports, clients, family/friends, and
mixed/other raters. Each rater completes the Bar-On EQ-360 assessment concerning a
particular subject and the subject completes the Bar-On EQ-i self-report instrument. The
results are compared to those of the various rater groups (MHS, 2006). The Bar-On EQ-
360 may have provided a better gauge of the correlation between supervisor and
subordinate emotional intelligence by examining each participant from the perspective of
the other. Future research may be well advised to consider this possibility.

Another alternative instrument that may have garnered statistically significant
correlations between the study variables is the Mayer, Salovey, and Caruso Emotional
Intelligence Test (MSCEIT). The MSCEIT is an active task-based instrument consisting
of a 141-item test that measures how well people perform tasks and solve emotional
problems on eight tasks, which are divided into four classes or branches of abilities
including (a) perceiving emotions, (b) facilitating thought, (c) understanding emotions,
and (d) managing emotions.

The MSCEIT measures perception of emotion by having people rate how much a
particular emotion is being expressed in either a picture of a face expressing a
basic emotion or in a picture of a design or landscape. Emotional facilitation of
thought is measured by asking people to describe emotional sensations and their

parallels to other sensory modalities and by having people assimilate predetermined mood into their thought processes concerning a fictional character. Understanding emotions is measured by asking people how emotions blend to form more complex emotions and how emotional reactions change over time. Finally, the MSCEIT measures emotion management by having test-takers choose effective ways to manage private emotions and the emotions of others in hypothetical situations (Brackett & Mayer, 2004, p. 197).

Mayer, Caruso, and Salovey (2000) make a strong argument for the use of an ability-based test instrument regarding emotional intelligence as an actual intelligence (Gardner, 1983, 1993, 1999, Thorndike, 1920). They present the view that ability testing of emotional intelligence will correspond to the actual capacity of a person to perform well at mental task rather than measuring one's belief or perception of how well they are able to perform those mental tasks (Mayer, Caruso, & Salovey, 2000).

The presentation of three succinct tests of emotional intelligence that include ability, self-report, and informant approaches to measurement. Mayer, Caruso, and Salovey (2000) expressed the following view regarding these three measures of emotional intelligence:

Tests of emotional intelligence that examine outcomes (such as leadership or teamwork) or noncognitive traits (such as assertiveness or impulse control) seem to tap a dimension of personality that is different from the idea of an intelligence. Such content may be more similar to existing personality models or scales. (p. 338)

Future researchers may wish to consider the possibility that an ability test of emotional intelligence may provide a better measure of the correlational effects of the test variables in similar studies than does the self-reporting instrument. It is the contention of this researcher that future researchers consider using the MSCEIT due to the task-based format of this instrument and its flexibility to report group findings as well as individual scores.

Another consideration and reflection regarding the lack of correlation between the study variables could possibly be the lack of random selection of the study participants. As previously indicated in both Chapters 3 and 4, it became necessary to abandon the randomly selected sample of sergeants and their respective subordinate patrol officers due to lack of participation on the part of the officers. It was surmised that a possible issue related to the lack of responsiveness of the officers may have been related to the fact that the officers are over-tested and if they are not required to submit to testing they are motivated to participate.

Chapter 4 identified the similarities of the sergeants in both the randomly selected sample and the convenience sample. It must be noted that the convenience sample's Officers' Mean Total EQ-i score of 100.26 was substantially closer to the randomly selected sample's Sergeants' Mean Total EQ-i of 102.05 than it was to the convenience sample's Sergeant's Mean Total EQ-i score of 107.23. These differences could offer an explanation for the final results of the study. Thus, had the randomly selected officers elected to participate, the results of the study could have been different and perhaps demonstrated a statistically significant correlational effect on the data.

An added consideration should be noted regarding the lack of complete pairing between the sergeants and officers. This too could provide further explanations for the lack of significance found in this study. Data were collected from two sergeants who were not paired with any officers. The officers supervised by these sergeants elected not to participate in the study. Data were collected from four officers who were not paired with their sergeant. The sergeant in this case chose not to participate in the study as well.

The pairing of the sergeants and their respective subordinates was a critical factor for this specific study. In order to determine if a sergeant's emotional intelligence level was correlated to the emotional intelligence level of subordinate officers it became necessary to pair the sergeant with his or her respective subordinates. Failure to make this connection between the sergeants and officers limited the efficacy of the results derived from the study. Future research, in order to avoid these pitfalls, could possibly be initiated by the top administrators of the organization making participation mandatory rather than voluntary in nature.

This researcher would be remiss not to point out an unexpected phenomenon that occurred with this research study. This researcher made an assumption that the patrol sergeants within this study would have contact with their subordinates either once a day or several times daily in the context of supervising. This researcher was informed by several participants, both sergeants and officers, that this assumption was false. In actuality, the supervising sergeants may only have contact with their subordinate officers a few times a week or possibly even once a week at best. The supposition that the supervisor's emotionally intelligent behavior might be modeled by or inculcated into the subordinate officer's modus operandi of emotional response was severely limited. This issue may also assist in the explanation of why there existed no statistically significant correlations between the emotional intelligence of the patrol sergeant and the subordinate officers.

This study does not diminish the importance and validity of emotional intelligence regarding the theoretical basis that it "is a cross-section of interrelated emotional and social competencies, skills and facilitators that determine how effectively we understand and express ourselves, understand others and relate with them, and cope with daily demands" (Bar-On, 2000, p. 3). Data from this study demonstrated that a sergeant with high EQ-i scores could be the supervisor of officers with lower EQ-i scores which indicated a need for improvement. Data collected also indicated the inverse to be true with this sample as well. A limited conclusion may be advanced, relative to the data ascertained in this specific study, which may suggest that, within this specific organization, a supervisor's emotional intelligence has no direct correlation to the emotional intelligence of his or her supervisee. This limited conclusion is contingent upon the lack of exact pairing of the sergeants and their subordinates as well as the limited amount of supervisory contact time with each officer.

The perspective that emotional intelligence is specific to the individual is consistently reinforced in the literature. A large portion of emotional intelligence research makes reference to reporting test results that clearly indicate the "individual or person" as the primary target of inquiry (Bar-On, 2005, 2000, 1997a; Bar-On & Parker, 2000; Brackett & Mayer, 2004; Caruso & Salovey, 2004; Cherniss, 2001; Cooper & Sawaf, 1997; Gardner & Stough, 2002; Higgs & Aitken, 2003; Mayer & Salovey, 2004; Mayer, Caruso, & Sitarenios, 2004; Salovey & Mayer, 2004; Salovey & Shuyter, 1997). Salovey and Mayer (2004, p. 17) have indicated that "the *person* [italics added] with emotional intelligence can be thought of as having attained at least a limited form of positive mental health. These *individuals* [italics added] are aware of their own feelings and those of others."Bar-On (1997a, p.1) stated that "to measure emotional intelligence is to measure *one's* [italics added] 'common sense' and ability to get along in the world."

Recent research has recently flourished regarding the concept of group emotional intelligence and its measurement (Cherniss, 2001; Druskat & Wolff, 2001a, 2001b; Hamme, 2003; Jordan, Ashkanasy, Härtel, & Hooper, 2002; Moriarty & Buckley, 2003; Stubbs, 2005; Yost & Tucker, 2000). Although the emphasis is directed toward the evaluation of group emotional intelligence, it appears that individual team members were the critical connection to group emotional intelligence.

Moriarty and Buckley (2003) concluded that training a group in emotional intelligence responses established skills that allow team members to understand their own styles of emotional interactions, handle emotions in the workplace, and increase their *individual* [italics added] level of self-awareness and self-concept. The outcome of these positive skills enhanced both the *individual* [italics added] human potential and group potential thereby benefiting the organization.

If emotional intelligence is related specifically to the individual then does group emotional intelligence really exist? Caruso and Salovey (2004) as well as Kelly and Barsade (2001) discussed the "emotional contagion" effect being used as an effective tool by emotionally intelligence leaders or a group member to motivate people toward a common goal or positively or negatively impacting the emotional state of other members of a specific group.

Yost and Tucker (2000) reported positively correlated results regarding the independent variable of emotional intelligence to the dependent variables of team performance, problem solving, and project grade. However, the results may have been skewed by the relatively small sample size (n = 73) and the lack of randomization in the study subjects. Moriarty and Buckley (2003) contended in their research that their experimental group, using group processes to build team skills, resolve internal differences, and accomplish group goals enhanced their emotional intelligence levels significantly from pre-test to post-test intervals. The touted enhancements did not reach a level of statistical significance to validate their hypothesis.

Hamme (2003) developed a group emotional intelligence test instrument based upon Druskat and Wolff (2001) conceptualization of group emotional intelligence. In the current literature there are no studies that have applied this instrument other than Hamme's (2003) study.

Jordan, Ashkanasy, Härtel, and Hooper (2002) initiated a study that employed the Workgroup Emotional Intelligence Profile, Version 3 (WEIP-3) which was specifically designed to profile the emotional intelligence of individuals in work groups. Analysis of the study results suggested that low emotional intelligence groups do not perform well in comparison to high emotional intelligence groups; however, over time the low emotional intelligence groups may perform as well high emotional intelligence groups.

Based upon the lack of research studies validating the concept of group emotional intelligence and integrated with the results of this study, could the assertion be made that group emotional intelligence does not exist? It would appear that group emotional intelligence is merely the combination of the emotional intelligence levels of each *individual* [italics added] group member and does not coalesce into a separate entity.

Summary

The primary finding derived from this research was that the patrol sergeant's emotional intelligence level was not correlated to the emotional intelligence level of the officers that he or she supervised. Emotional intelligence appears to be an individual attribute that may not directly impact the manner in which a sergeant interacts with his or her subordinates, peers, superiors, or the general public. Emotional intelligence may impact the way and manner in which an officer interacts and deals with his or her peers, supervisor, or the general public that he or she serves, but may not be related to the individuals with whom he or she supervises. Due to the lack of statistical significance in the correlational coefficients of this study, the null hypothesis was retained.

Emotional intelligence is, nevertheless, a very important attribute, skill, or capacity that can serve the police officer and police supervisor very well in the performance of his or her duties. Individuals exhibiting functional or high levels of emotional intelligence are capable of managing their own emotions, understanding and responding appropriately to the emotions of others, and exhibiting flexibility and adaptability within their personal and professional lives (Bar-On, 1997a; Salovey & Mayer, 2004).

This study was built on establishing a case that there existed a connection between the emotional intelligence of a patrol sergeant and the emotional intelligence of the officers that he or she supervised. The foundation of this study was based on two precepts: 1) emotional intelligence is an attribute that can be taught by modeling behavior; and 2) emotional intelligence may be learned through social interactions between supervisor and supervisee. Previous research has not considered the significance of either of these principles. Therefore, the contribution of this study, to the body of literature regarding emotional intelligence, may be the fact that neither principle was demonstrated within the confines of this research project.

Mayer and Salovey (2004) indicated "Emotional skills begin in the home with good parent-child interaction. Parents help children identify and label their emotions, to respect their feelings, and to begin to connect them to social situations. This process may succeed to a greater or lesser degree in each home" (p. 43). The significance of the informal relationships between a child and a teacher, wherein the teacher serves in the role of an important and potentially wise adult model, presents an excellent venue for teaching appropriate behavior and emotional responses.

This study subsumed the process of modeling behavior that presented the perceived appropriate emotional response would also occur in the informal relationships formulated between a patrol sergeant and his or her subordinate officers. This assumption was not true in this research. The results propounded by this study appear to beseech the question – why was this reasoning flawed? Critical reflection regarding the answer to this question brought forth a number of additional questions for investigation. Do police officers actually emulate the behavior of their supervisor? If they do, what are the prerequisites for emulation? Does the fact that a supervisor is a member of the organization's administration limit their effectiveness in modeling behavior, particularly those relative to emotional responses? Do adult police officers tend to base their emotional responses on parental modeling that ensued during the formative years of their lives? Do police officers formulate their own emotional responses based upon previous life experiences?

It is obvious that additional research is needed surrounding the issues of emotional intelligence and polices officers. The literature is substantially lacking relative to police officers and emotional intelligence. The policing profession is a singular profession wherein appropriate emotional responses, particularly during highly stressful situations, may reap tremendous rewards of saving lives and enhancing the image of a professional constabulary. These two reasons are substantial motivations for continued research and exploration into the field of emotional intelligence and the policing profession.

CHAPTER 6

SUMMARY AND IMPLICATIONS

Police work, by its very nature, can produce conflict and highly charged emotional circumstances. Police officers are required to maintain calm and self-control, even in the face of danger. Police officers have typically looked to senior officers or supervisors as a model for the way and manner in which these situations should be handled and controlled. It is certainly conceivable to believe that a sergeant exhibiting high levels of emotional intelligence could provide a positive role model for his or her subordinates to emulate. The results of this exploratory study, however, failed to demonstrate a correlational relationship between the emotional intelligence of sergeants and the emotional intelligence of their subordinate officers.

There were no statistically significant relationships among the variables of this research. Empirical research related to the examination of correlational relationships between the emotional intelligence of one generalized group and the emotional intelligence of another generalized group was not found in the current body of literature. Does the emotional intelligence, either high or low, of a supervisor have a correlational connection to the emotional intelligence, either high or low, of the supervisor's subordinates? Research regarding this particular concern could provide supporting data to either establish or refute the concept of group emotional intelligence. It could also provide added value to the concepts of behavior modeling and training relative to emotional intelligence. Organizational and leadership research would also benefit from studies related to the topic of emotional intelligence of supervisors and subordinates and the impact that one may have on the other. A void in the literature relevant to this topic currently exists and thus denotes a need for future research and exploration.

The failure of this research to identify correlations between the variables of supervisor emotional intelligence and subordinate emotional intelligence suggests a need for additional research in the areas of policing, such as police leadership, organizational behavior, and stress management, as well as the subject of emotional intelligence which would include the impact of emotional intelligence levels of supervisors and supervisees, behavior modeling of emotional intelligence, and the existence of group emotional intelligence.

Additionally, the area of transformational leadership and emotional intelligence could benefit from additional research in the areas previously indicated. Transformational leadership was briefly discussed in the Chapter 2 of this study and raised the question of whether emotionally intelligent leaders are just transformational leaders in a new packaging. It is evident from the literature that emotional intelligence and its affect on organizational and transformational leadership has been studied very closely in recent years (Barling, Slater, & Kelloway, 2000; Buford, 2001; Gardner & Stough, 2001; Higgs & Aitken, 2003; Langley, 2000; Malek, 2000; Palmer, Walls, Burgess, & Stough, 2000; Weinberger, 2003; Wong & Law, 2002) as well as books written on the subject (Caruso & Salovey, 2004; Cherniss & Adler, 2000; Cherniss & Goleman, 2001; Goleman, 1998). Results regarding its impact have been mixed; however, there does appear to be correlations between high emotional intelligence and transformational leadership qualities (Barling, Slater, & Kelloway, 2000).

Why is transformational leadership relevant to this particular study? A study conducted by Palmer, Wall, Burgess, and Stough (2001) found that transformational leaders' capacity to motivate and inspire others was significantly correlated to both the ability to monitor and manage emotions in themselves and others. If a sergeant is a transformational leader then his or her ability to monitor and manage emotions is enhanced and could potentially increase the desire of his or her subordinates to emulate the behavior expressed by their leader. Additional research directed toward the enhancement of transformational leadership qualities and techniques and the impact of emotional intelligence levels of supervisors on their subordinates could yield potentially significant results.

Does emotional intelligence constitute an important construct in the policing profession? Ricca's (2003) research as well as the research of Bar-On, Brown, Kirkcaldy, and Thomé (2000) demonstrated that emotional intelligence does contribute to the reducing burnout and controlling stress in police officers respectively. It would also appear that emotional intelligence would aid police officers in responding appropriately to critical incident situations that are highly charged and extremely volatile. Bar-On (1997a) addressed the issue of predicting aggressive behaviors in the workplace with a specific case study regarding a 31-year-old police who was dismissed from the police department due to a tendency to exercise excessive force in the line of duty. Bar-On (1997a) indicated that the officer had four complaints lodged against him over a period of two and a half years wherein he had used excessive force. Three of the four people filing complaints required hospitalization following the officer's actions. Bar-On described the officer's EQ-i results with the following assessment:

> The officer's total EQ score (89) is situated close to the lower limits of the normal range. A low Empathy score (EM = 70), together with a low Social Responsibility score (RE = 84), most likely means that his irresponsible negative behavior is related to a lack of understanding and appreciation of how other people feel. He has a somewhat limited problem-solving ability (PS = 84) and

could be having difficulty in "sizing up" the situation (RT = 89). This whole

picture is clearly exacerbated by his difficulty in dealing with stressful situations

(ST = 79) and, especially, by his serious lack of impulse control (IC = 68). (Bar-

On, 1997a, p. 58)

Although, this case study may be considered to be anecdotal, it nevertheless

illustrates the potential of use by law enforcement officials and administrators to

effectively test and enhance emotional intelligence among the police officers that serve

our nation's citizenry. Enhancing emotional intelligence in police officers would

therefore appear to be a desirable option for law enforcement administrators and

agencies.

In this final chapter, the implications of this study will be discussed in relationship

to theory and future research initiatives as well as practical implications.

Theoretical Implications and Future Research

Although the results of this research failed to attain statistical significance

regarding the variables explored, it still suggests important implications for the

theoretical ambits of emotional intelligence.

Emotional Intelligence

There exists no research in the body of literature surrounding emotional

intelligence demonstrating a relationship between the emotional intelligence of a

supervisor and the emotional intelligence of his or her subordinates. Does the lack of

statistical significance within this study suggest that such a relationship does not exist and

therefore precludes the need to examine this relationship?

It is this researcher's contention that further research needs to be conducted to

determine if such a relationship actually exists or fails to exist. Is emotional intelligence a concept relative only to the influences of the individual psyche and has no connection to the influences of supervisors or mentors in a person's life? Further examination regarding the influence of others is needed to satisfy the void in the literature left by this unanswered question.

Mayer and Salovey (2004) suggested that a person acquires the rudiments of their emotional skills, for better or worse, from the interaction with their parents. They also suggested that it was possible for a refinement of these emotional skills to come from the informal relationships of student-teacher interactions (Mayer & Salovey, 2004). During the formative school years, children may actually emulate the action of their role models relative to emotional behavior and demeanor. These observations or generalizations seem to validate the proposal that emotional intelligence can be taught.

Is emotional intelligence dependent upon the recipient of these "lessons" being aware of what constitutes a proper emotional response and then being cognizant of and ready to inculcate these changes? Ashkanasy and Dasborough (2003) suggested that individuals who experience an interest or awareness of emotions and emotional intelligence could lead to a prediction of team performance.

Future research may consider pre-testing the emotional intelligence of patrol sergeants (supervisors) and the emotional intelligence of their patrol officers (subordinates), followed by training to enhance the emotional intelligence level of the sergeants, and then conduct a post-test of the emotional intelligence level of the sergeants and their respective officers. Analyses may then be conducted to determine if a change occurred in the emotional intelligence score of the officers as a result of the change in the sergeants' emotional intelligence score.

Practical Implications

In this section, implications for using emotional intelligence in the policing profession are discussed.

Emotional Intelligence in the Policing Profession

Bar-On (1997a) provided a case study using the EQ-i in predicting and explaining physically aggressive behavior and excessive force in the line of duty on the part of a 31-year-old police officer. Ricca (2003) demonstrated an inverse relationship between high emotional intelligence and on-the-job burnout for police officers in her study.

Although there exists little in the way of research regarding emotional intelligence and the police, it would seem that the concept of emotional intelligence could provide police administration a new tool for the selection and training of police officers throughout the world. Police officers are constantly faced with circumstances involving volatile emotions and conflict. Being capable of appraising one's own emotions, assessing the emotions of others, and responding appropriately in order to reduce the necessity of force is an attribute that all police administrators and officers should embrace. The emotionally intelligent constabulary could possibly aid in the reduction of potentially lethal conflicts that might lead to the injury or death of an officer or citizen.

It is necessary to establish a disclaimer to the following suppositions promulgated by this researcher. None of the benefits indicated in this section have been validated by scientific inquiry and are therefore merely conjecture on the part of the researcher. Emotionally intelligent police officers could potentially enjoy the added benefit of being better able to resist the pressures and burden of stress. Emotionally intelligent police officers would be capable of resolving stressful situations in their personal and professional lives; thereby, limiting the potential dilemmas of poor physical health, mental illness, and divorce. Emotionally intelligent police officers would more likely enjoy their jobs and feel a sense of self-actualization in their career choice of policing. These benefits could translate to increased productivity, decreased use of sick leave, an enhancement in the professional image projected to the general public, and an increase in the perception of professional and personal integrity of the police by the general public.

A similar disclaimer, like the one previously indicated, is attached to the views submitted regarding future research options and potential results. Future research may also examine police agencies to determine if emotionally intelligent police officers are less likely to use excessive force, are less likely to have incidences of defendant's resisting arrest, and are less likely to be named in law suits for violations of a defendant's civil rights. Based upon the results of this future research, law enforcement administrators may be able to dramatically reduce the occurrence of these problems that tarnish the professionalism of police officers throughout the nation.

The potential to influence the emotional intelligence levels of numerous officers by enhancing the emotional intelligence of a supervisor would have a certain appeal to the fiscally responsible police administrator. If it is determined that the enhancement of the emotional intelligence of a police supervisor would have a direct correlation to the emotional intelligence of his or her subordinate officers' emotional intelligence, then police supervisors could receive training in emotional intelligence at a fraction of the cost to an entire department yet yield exponential results in the benefits of emotional intelligence within the police agency.

Another consideration for future research could be the consideration of examining the emotional intelligence of patrol training officers and the novice officers that they are responsible for training. The significant face-to-face contact of the training officer with the "rookie" officer could possibly provide a very significant contribution to the body of literature regarding the influence and impact the senior officer has over the emotional intelligence of the neophyte officer.

All of these potential benefits provide a basis for continued research in the area of emotional intelligence and the policing profession. A significant deficiency currently exists in the research literature surrounding the police and emotional intelligence. Contributions to reducing the paucity of research in this area are greatly needed. Does the emotionally intelligent police officer actually provide the articulated benefits discussed in this chapter? A speculative answer of yes is assumed by this researcher; however, only the results of solid quantitative and qualitative research can accurately resolve the question.

Recommendations for Law Enforcement Practice

Based upon the results of this specific project, the researcher has considered the implications and derived potential recommendations for use of emotional intelligence in the field of policing. Four recommendations are introduced by this researcher regarding 1) the use of an ability-based emotional intelligence assessment instrument that may be better able to provide relevant data to the police administrator regarding his or her line personnel and supervisors, 2) the use of experiments within the ranks of supervisors to determine if enhancement of emotional intelligence will have a quantifiable effect on subordinate personnel, 3) the use of emotional intelligence enhancement training to reduce police burnout and occupational stress, and 4) the use of and participation in emotional intelligence research projects directed toward the policing profession.

Based upon the findings of this study, police departments and administrators should consider the use of an ability-based emotional intelligence assessment instrument as a means of accurately measuring the emotional intelligence capacity of its officers and supervisors. It became clear to this researcher that an ability-based emotional intelligence instrument may more accurately depict the capabilities of both patrol sergeants and their respective subordinate officers regarding emotional intelligence. An active task-based approach to the emotional intelligence assessment instrument may more appropriately address the emotional intelligence capacity of the police officer than does the self-reporting, noncognitive traits-based instrument (Mayer, Caruso, & Salovey, 2000).

Police administrators should consider the application of pretest-posttest experiments designed to determine if enhancing the emotional intelligence of a supervisor will have statistically significant results on his or her subordinate officers. The application of a pretest to determine the emotional intelligence levels of experimental and control groups of sergeants and subordinates followed by an enhancement program of emotional intelligence for the experimental group sergeants and concluding with a posttest to determine the variances between the experimental and control groups of sergeants and subordinates could provide valuable information regarding any potential links to emotional intelligence of sergeants and the modeling of behavior by subordinate officers. The results of this study did not address this issue. In retrospect, the consideration of an experimental design for analysis of this project may have yielded a more thorough analysis of the problem and a critical set of data to weigh the results.

Based also upon the limited research cited, emotional intelligence training should potentially be considered by police administrators as a mechanism to reduce the effects of burnout and occupational stress relative to officers within the policing profession. Ricca (2003) indicated that an inverse relationship existed between emotional intelligence and burnout within the ranks of her study sample. The higher the emotional intelligence of an officer, the less likely he or she would be to experience burnout. Bar-On, Kirkcaldy, and Thomé (2000) examined occupational stress relative to police officers, child-care workers, and educators in mental health care. The results of this study suggested that police officers achieved higher scores on emotional stability and positive affect than did the care workers. The interpretation of these results would suggest that police officers tend to be more capable of dealing with stressful issues based upon the training that they receive as well as a regular exposure to these situations.

Emotional intelligence should also be considered by police agencies as a training tool used in the development of police officers currently engaged in the policing profession. The enhancement of emotional intelligence within the constabulary could serve to personally enrich the lives of officers currently employed with an agency, while at the same time garner an improved perception of professionalism from the citizenry that they serve. Future longitudinal research may possibly consider the correlational effect of enhanced emotional intelligence training on citizen complaints of police personnel. Additionally, future researchers could explore the effects of emotional intelligence on police officer behavior in various critical incident situations.

The final recommendation is a call for all law enforcement officers and administrators to reduce their defensive posture and inhibitions toward participation in research. Increasing the body of knowledge surrounding the policing profession can produce significant benefits for the officers and agencies participating as well as the police profession in general. Research studies regarding areas like emotional intelligence can improve the understanding of various phenomenon and can directly contribute to better policing.

Summary

Emotional intelligence has been established as a viable concept in the field of psychology, education, and organizational behavior. Salovey and Mayer (2004) coined the term of emotional intelligence in 1990 and Bar-On (1997a) developed the EQ-i as an instrument to measure this construct in 1995. During the past decade a multitude of studies have been instigated to examine this theory relative to an individual's emotional intelligence; however, no studies have addressed the issue of a whether a supervisor's emotional intelligence will have an impact on the emotional intelligence of his or her subordinate.

Although this study failed to demonstrate a significant relationship between the emotional intelligence of a patrol sergeant and his or her subordinate officers, it has succeeded in demonstrating a need for future exploration and research in the field of emotional intelligence and behavior modeling. Emotional intelligence may provide an important component in selecting and training police officers of the future.

REFERENCES

Abraham, R. (1998). Emotional intelligence in organizations: A conceptualization. *Genetic, Social, and General Psychology Monographs, 125*, 209–224.

Adams, T.F. (2004). *Police field operations* (6th ed.). Upper Saddle River, NJ: Pearson/Prentice Hall.

Alderson, W. (1985). *Value of the person: Theory r concept.* Pittsburgh, PA: Value of the Person Press.

Anderson, T.D. (2000). *Every officer is a leader: Transforming leadership in police, justice, and public safety.* Boca Raton, FL: St. Lucie Press.

Argyris, C. (1964). *Integrating the individual and the organization.* New York: Wiley.

Argyris, C. (1982). *Reasoning, learning and action: Individual and organizational.* San Francisco: Jossey-Bass.

Ashkanasy, N.M., & Dasborough, M.T. (2003). Emotional awareness and emotional intelligence in leadership training [Electronic edition]. *Journal of Education for Business,* 18-22.

Bardzil, P., & Slaski, M. (2003). Emotional intelligence: Fundamental competencies for enhanced service provision [Electronic edition]. *Managing Service Quality, 13*(2), 97-104.

Bagshaw, M. (2000). Emotional intelligence – training people to be affective so they can be effective [Electronic edition]. *Industrial and Commercial Training, 32*(2), 61-65.

Barling, J., Slater, F., & Kelloway, E. K. (2000). Transformational leadership and emotional intelligence: An exploratory study [Electronic edition]. *Leadership & Organization Development Journal, 21*(3), 157-161.

Bar-On, R. (2005) *The Bar-On model of emotional-social intelligence*. Retrieved March

25, 2005, from http://www.eiconsortium.org/research/baron_model_of_

emotional_social_intelligence.htm

Bar-On. R. (2000). Emotional intelligence and social intelligence: Insights from the

emotional quotient inventory. In R. Bar-On & J.D.A. Parker (Eds.), *The*

handbook of emotional intelligence: Theory, development, assessment, and

application at home, school, and in the workplace (pp. 363-388). San Francisco:

Jossey-Bass.

Bar-On, R. (1997a). *BarOn emotional quotient inventory (eq-i): Technical manual*.

Toronto, Canada: Multi-Health Systems.

Bar-On, R. (1997b). *BarOn emotional quotient inventory: User's manual*. Toronto,

Canada: Multi-Health Systems.

Bar-On, R., Brown, J.M., Kirkcaldy, B.D., & Thomé, E.P. (2000). Emotional expression

and implications for occupational stress; an application of the emotional quotient

inventory (eq-i) [Electronic edition]. *Personality and Individual Differences, 28*,

1107-1118.

Bar-On, R., & Parker, J.D.A. (2000). *The handbook of emotional intelligence: Theory,*

development, assessment, and application at home, school, and in the workplace.

San Francisco: Jossey-Bass.

Bass, B.M. & Avolio, B.J. (1994). *Improving organizational effectiveness through*

transformational leadership. Thousand Oaks, CA: Sage Publications

Bassi, L.J., Benson, G., & Cheney, S. (1996). The top ten trends [Electronic edition].

Training and Development, 50(11), 28-43.

Bennett, W.W., & Hess, K.M. (2004). *Management and supervision in law enforcement* (4th ed.). Belmont, CA: Wadsworth.

Bennis, W.G. (1961). Revisionist theory of leadership. *Harvard Business Review, 39*(1), 26-37.

Blake, R.R., & Mouton, J.S. (1964). *The managerial grid.* Houston, TX: Gulf.

Blanchard, K., & Hersey, P. (1982). *Management of organizational behavior: Utilizing human resources.* Englewood Cliffs, NJ: Prentice-Hall.

Bohm, R. M., & Haley, K. N. (2005). *Introduction to criminal justice* (4th ed.). New York: McGraw-Hill.

Bolman, L.G., & Deal, T.E. (1997). *Reframing organizations: Artistry, choice, and leadership* (2nd ed.). San Francisco: Jossey-Bass.

Boyatzis, R.E., & Oosten, E.V. (2002, July 10). Developing emotionally intelligent organizations. Retrieved March 11, 2005, from http://www.eiconsortium.org/research/developing_emotionally_intelligent_organizations.htm .

Brackett, M.A., & Mayer, J.D. (2004). Convergent, discriminant, and incremental validity of competing measures of emotional intelligence. In P. Salovey, M.A. Brackett & J.D. Mayer (Eds.), *Emotional intelligence: Key readings on the Mayer and Salovey model* (pp. 195-219). Port Chester, NY: Dude Publishing.

Brooks, J.K. (2002). *Emotional competencies of leaders: A comparison of managers in a financial organization by performance level.* Unpublished doctoral dissertation, North Carolina State University, Raleigh.

Brown, J.M., & Campbell, E.A. (1990). Sources of occupational stress in police work. *Work and Stress, 4*(4), 305-318.

Buford, B.A. (2001). Management effectiveness, personality, leadership, and emotional

   intelligence: A study of the validity evidence of the emotional quotient inventory

   (eq-i). *Dissertation Abstracts International, 62*, 12B. (UMI No. 3034082).

Carmeli, A. (2003). The relationship between emotional intelligence and work attitudes,

   behavior and outcomes: An examination among senior managers [Electronic

   edition]. *Journal of Managerial Psychology, 18*(8), 788-813.

Caruso, D.R., & Salovey, P. (2004). *The emotionally intelligent manager: How to develop

   and use the four key emotional skills of leadership.* San Francisco: Jossey-Bass.

Champion, D.J. (2003). *Administration of criminal justice: Structure, function, and process.*

   Upper Saddle River, NJ: Prentice Hall.

Cherniss, C. (2001). Emotional intelligence and organizational effectiveness. In C. Cherniss

   & D. Goleman (Eds.), *The emotionally intelligence workplace: How to select for,*

   measure, and improve emotional intelligence in individuals, groups, and

   organizations (pp. 3-12). San Francisco: Jossey-Bass.

Cherniss, C. (2000, April 15). *Emotional intelligence: What it is and why it matters.* Paper

   presented at the Annual Meeting of the Society for Industrial and Organizational

   Psychology. Paper retrieved February 25, 2005, from

   http://www.eiconsortium.org/research/what_is_emotional_intelligence.htm

Cherniss, C., & Adler, M. (2000). *Promoting emotional intelligence in organizations:*

   Guidelines to help you design, implement, and evaluate effective programs.

   Alexandria, VA: ASTD Press.

Cherniss, C., & Caplan, R.D. (2001). A case study for implementing emotional intelligence

   programs in organizations [Electronic edition]. *Journal of Organizational*

   Excellence, (Winter), 73-85.

Childre, D.L., & Cryer, B. (1999). *From chaos to coherence: Advancing emotional and organizational intelligence through inner quality management.* Woburn, MA: Butterworth-Heinemann.

Cooper, R.K., & Sawaf, A. (1997). *Executive eq: Emotional intelligence in leadership and organizations.* New York: Grosset/Putnam.

Crank, J.P., & Caldero, M. (1991). The production of occupational stress in medium-sized police agencies: A study of line officers in eight municipal departments [Electronic edition]. *Journal of Criminal Justice, 19,* 339-349.

Cronbach, L. J. (1960). *Essentials of psychological testing* (2nd ed.). New York: Harper & Row.

Druskat, V.U., & Wolff, S.B. (2001a). Group emotional intelligence and its influence on group effectiveness. In C. Cherniss & D. Goleman (Eds.), *The emotionally intelligence workplace: How to select for, measure, and improve emotional intelligence in individuals, groups, and organizations* (pp. 132-155). San Francisco: Jossey-Bass.

Druskat, V.U., & Wolff, S.B. (2001b). Building emotional intelligence of groups [Electronic edition]. *Harvard Business Review, 79*(3), 81–90.

Dulewicz, V., Higgs, M., Slaski, M. (2003). Measuring emotional intelligence: Content, construct and criterion-related validity [Electronic edition]. *Journal of Managerial Psychology, 18*(5), 405-420.

Dulewicz, V., & Higgs, M. (2000). Emotional intelligence: A review and evaluation study [Electronic edition]. *Journal of Managerial Psychology, 15*(4), 341-372.

Dulewicz, V. & Higgs, M. (1999). Can emotional intelligence be measured and developed [Electronic edition]? *Leadership & Organization Development Journal, 20*(5), 242-252.

Emmerling, R.J., & Goleman, D. (2003, October). Emotional intelligence: Issues and common misunderstandings. Retrieved March 3, 2005, from http://www.eiconsortium.org/research/ei_issues_and_common_misunderstandings.hm .

Engel, R.S. (2003). Police officers' attitudes, behavior, and supervisory influences: An analysis of problem solving [Electronic edition]. *Criminology, 41*(2), 131-166.

Engel, R.S. (2002). Patrol officer supervision in the community policing era [Electronic edition]. *Journal of Criminal Justice, 30*(1), 51-64.

Engel, R.S. (2001). Supervisory styles of patrol sergeants and lieutenants [Electronic edition]. *Journal of Criminal Justice, 29*(4), 341-355.

Engel, R.S., & Worden, R. E. (2003). Police officers' attitudes, behavior and supervisory influences: An analysis of problem solving. *Criminology, 41*(1), 131 – 166.

Evans, B.J., Coman, G.J., & Stanley, R.O. (1992). The police personality: Type a behavior and trait anxiety [Electronic edition]. *Journal of Criminal Justice, 20*, 429-441.

Federal Bureau of Investigation. (n.d.). *Crime in the united states : Section vi – law enforcement personnel* (Uniform Crime Report – 2002). Retrieved December 28, 2005 from http://www.fbi.gov/ucr/cius_02/html/web/lawenforcement/lawenforcement.html

Feldman, D.A. (1999). *The handbook of emotionally intelligent leadership: Inspiring others to achieve results.* Falls Church, VA: Leadership Performance Solutions Press.

Fiedler, F.E. (1967). *A theory of leadership effectiveness.* New York: McGraw-Hill.

Gardner, H. (1999). *Intelligence reframed: Multiple Intelligences for the 21ˢᵗ century*. New York: BasicBooks.

Gardner, H. (1993). *Multiple intelligences: The theory in practice*. New York: Basic Books.

Gardner, H. (1983). *Frames of mind*. New York: Basic Books.

Gardner, L., & Stough, C. (2002). Examining the relationship between leadership and emotional intelligence in senior level managers [Electronic edition]. *Leadership & Organization Development Journal, 23*(2), 68-78.

George, J.M. (2000). Emotions and leadership: The role of emotional intelligence [Electronic edition]. *Human Relations, 53*(8), 1027-1055.

Goleman, D. (2001). Emotional intelligence: Issues in paradigm building. In C. Cherniss & D. Goleman (Eds.), *The emotionally intelligence workplace: How to select for, measure, and improve emotional intelligence in individuals, groups, and organizations* (pp. 13-26). San Francisco: Jossey-Bass.

Goleman, D. (1998). *Working with emotional intelligence*. New York: Bantam Books.

Goleman, D. (1995). *Emotional intelligence*. New York: Bantam Books.

Hamme, C.L. (2003). Group emotional intelligence: The research and development of an assessment instrument. *Dissertation Abstracts International, 64,* 09B, 4663.

Harrison, B. (2001, October). Policy and procedure: What new sergeants need to know. *Law and Order,49*(10), 151–153.

Hartsfield, M. K. (2003). The internal dynamics of transformational leadership: Effects of spirituality, emotional intelligence, and self-efficacy. *Dissertation Abstracts International, 64*(05B), 2440.

Hess, K.M., & Wrobleski, H.M. (1997). *Police operations: Theory and practice* (2ⁿᵈ ed.). St. Paul, MN: West Publishing.

Higgs, M., & Aitken, P. (2003). An exploration of the relationship between emotional

 intelligence and leadership potential [Electronic edition]. *Journal of Managerial*

 Psychology, 18(8), 814-823.

House, R. (1971, September 16). A path-goal model of leader effectiveness. *Administrative*

 Science Quarterly, 312-338.

Jacobs, R.L. (2001). Using human resource functions to enhance emotional intelligence.

 In C. Cherniss & D. Goleman (Eds.), *The emotionally intelligent workplace* (p. 159–

 171). San Francisco: Jossey-Bass.

Jacksonville Sheriff's Office. (2005). Retrieved March 21, 2005, from

 http://www.coj.net/Departments/Sheriffs+Office/Personnel/Police+Recruitment.htm

Jordan, P.J., Ashkanasy, N.M., Härtel, C.E.J., & Hooper, G.S. (2002). Workgroup emotional

 intelligence: Scale development and relationship to team process effectiveness and

 goal focus [Electronic edition]. *Human Resource Management Review 12* (2), 195-

 214.

Kelly, J. R., & Barsade, S. G. (2001). Mood and emotions in small groups and work teams

 [Electronic edition]. *Organizational Behavior and Human Decision Processes, 86*(1),

 99-130.

Kotter, J.P., & Cohen, D.S. (2002). *The heart of change: Real-life stories of how people*

 change their organizations. Boston: Harvard Business School Press.

Kram, K.E., & Cherniss, C. (2001). Developing emotional competence through relationships

 at work. In C. Cherniss & D. Goleman (Eds.), *The emotionally intelligent workplace,*

 (pp. 254-285). San Francisco: Jossey-Bass.

Langley, A. (2000). Emotional intelligence - a new evaluation for management development

 [Electronic edition]. *Career Development International, 5*(3), 177-183.

Lord, V. B. (1996). An impact of community policing: Reported stressors, social support, and strain among police officers in a changing police department [Electronic edition]. *Journal of Criminal Justice, 24*(6), 503-522.

Jaeger, A.J. (2001). *Emotional intelligence learning style, and academic performance of graduate students in professional schools.* Unpublished doctoral dissertation, New York University, New York City.

Johnson, P.R., & Indvik, J. (1999). Organizational benefits of having emotionally intelligent managers and employees [Electronic edition]. *Journal of Workplace Learning, 11*(3), 84-88.

Jordan, P. J., Ashkanasy, N. M., Hartel, C.E.J., and Hooper, G. S. (2002). Workgroup emotional intelligence: Scale development and relationship to team process effectiveness and goal focus [Electronic edition]. *Human Resource Management Review, 12*(2), 195-214.

Likert, R. (1967). *The human organization.* New York: McGraw-Hill.

Lippman, W. (1922). The mental age of Americans. *New Republic, 32*(412), 213–215.

Massey, H.E. (1999). The new leader's role: Engaging dialogue and emotional intelligency at entry for successful adaptive change. *Dissertation Abstracts International, 59,* 7-A, 2607.

Mastrofski, S., Parks, R., Reiss, A. Jr., & Worden, R. (July 1999). *Policing neighborhoods: A report from St. Petersburg* (US Department of Justice, NIJ No.184370). Washington, DC: Author

Mastrofski, S., Parks, R., Reiss, A. Jr., & Worden, R. (July 1999). *Policing neighborhoods: A report from Indianapolis* (US Department of Justice, NIJ No.184207). Washington, DC: Author

Malek, M. (2000). Relationship between emotional intelligence and collaborative conflict

    resolution styles. *Dissertation Abstracts International, 61*, 05B. (UMI No.

    9970564)

Mayer, J.D., Caruso, D.R., & Salovey, P. (2000). Selecting a measure of emotional

    intelligence: The case for ability scales. In R. Bar-On & J. D. A. Parker (Eds.),

    The handbook of emotional intelligence: Theory, development, assessment, and

    application at home, school, and in the workplace (pp. 320 - 342). San Francisco:

    Jossey-Bass.

Mayer, J.D., & Salovey, P. (2004). What is emotional intelligence? In P. Salovey, M.A.

    Brackett & J.D. Mayer (Eds.), *Emotional intelligence: Key readings on the Mayer*

    and Salovey model (pp. 29 – 59). Port Chester, NY: Dude Publishing.

Mayer, J.D., Salovey, P., Caruso, D.R., & Sitarenios, G. (2004). Measuring emotional

    intelligence with the msceit v2.0. In P. Salovey, M.A. Brackett & J.D. Mayer (Eds.),

    Emotional intelligence: Key readings on the Mayer and Salovey model (pp. 179-193).

    Port Chester, NY: Dude Publishing.

McGregor, D. (1966). *Leadership and motivation.* Cambridge, MA: MIT Press.

Miami Dade College. (2005). Retrieved March 21, 2005, from

    http://www.mdc.edu/north/f-bat/about_the_test.asp

Møller, C., & Powell, S. (2001). Emotional intelligence and the challenges of quality

    management today [Electronic edition]. *Leadership & Organization Development*

    Journal, 22(7), 341-344.

More, H.W., & Wegener, W.F. (1996). *Effective police supervision* (2nd ed.). Cincinnati, OH:

    Anderson Publishing.

Moriarty, P., & Buckley, F. (2003). Increasing team emotional intelligence through

　　process [Electronic edition]. *Journal of European Industrial Training, 27*(2),

　　98-110.

Multi-Health Systems, Inc. (MHS). (2006). Retrieved January 25, 2006 from

　　http://www.emotionalintelligencemhs.com/TechnicalBroch.asp.

Ouchi, W. (1981). *Theory z: How American business can meet the Japanese challenge.*

　　Reading, MA: Addison-Wesley.

Palmer, B., Walls, M., Burgess, Z., & Stough, C. (2001). Emotional intelligence and

　　effective leadership [Electronic edition]. *Leadership & Organization*

　　Development Journal, 22(1), 5-10.

Patterson, G.T. (2003). Examining the effects of coping and social support on work and

　　life stress among police officers [Electronic edition]. *Journal of Criminal Justice,*

　　31, 215-226.

Peak, K.J. (2004). *Justice administration: Police, courts, and corrections management*

　　(4th ed.). Upper Saddle River, NJ: Pearson/Prentice Hall.

Perrott, S.B., & Taylor, D.M. (1995). Attitudinal differences between police constables

　　and their supervisors: Potential influences of personality and work environment.

　　Criminal Justice and Behavior, 22, 326-339.

Pogrebin, M.R., & Poole, E.D. (1991). Police and tragic events: The management of

　　emotions [Electronic edition]. *Journal of Criminal Justice, 19*, 395-403.

Rahim, M.A., & Minors, P. (2003). Effects of emotional intelligence on concern for

　　quality and problem solving [Electronic edition]. *Managerial Auditing Journal,*

　　18(2), 150-155.

Ricca, D. (2003). Emotional intelligence, negative mood regulation expectancies, and professional burnout among police officers. *Dissertation Abstracts International, 64*, 09B. (UMI No. 3106382)

Rozell, E.J., Pettijohn, C.E., & Parker, R.S. (2002). An empirical evaluation of emotional intelligence: The impact on management development [Electronic edition]. *Journal of Management Development, 21*(4), 272-289.

Savery, L. K., Soutar, G.N., & Weaver, R. (1993). Stress and the police officer: Some West Australian evidence. *The Police Journal, 66*, 277-290.

Salovey, P., & Mayer, J.D. (2004). Emotional intelligence. In P. Salovey, M.A. Brackett & J.D. Mayer (Eds.), *Emotional intelligence: Key readings on the Mayer and Salovey model* (pp. 1 – 27). Port Chester, NY: Dude Publishing.

Salovey, P., & Shuyter, D.J. (1997). *Emotional development and emotional intelligence: Educational implications.* New York: Basic Books.

Schutte, N.S., Malouff, J.M., Hall, L.E., Haggerty, D.J, Cooper, J.T., Golden, C.J., et.al. (1998). Development and validation of a measure of emotional intelligence [Electronic edition]. *Personality and Individual Differences, 25*(2), 167-177.

Simmons, S., & Simmons, J.C. Jr. (1997). *Measuring emotional intelligence: The groundbreaking guide to applying the principles of emotional intelligence.* Arlington, TX: The Summit Publishing Group.

Sivanathan, N., & Fekken, G.C. (2002). Emotional intelligence, moral reasoning and transformational leadership [Electronic edition]. *Leadership & Organization, 23*(4),198-204.

Spearman, C. (1973). *The nature of 'intelligence' and the principles of cognition.* New York: Arno Press. [Reprint of 1923 edition]

Spearman, C. (1904). "General intelligence" objectively determined and measured. *American Journal of Psychology, 15*(2), 201-293.

Stephens, C., Long, N., & Miller, I. (1997). The impact of trauma and social support on posttraumatic stress disorder: A study of New Zealand police officers [Electronic edition]. *Journal of Criminal Justice, 25*(4), 303-314.

Stratton, J.G. (1984). *Police passages.* Manhattan Beach, CA: Glennon.

Sternberg, R.J. (1985). *Beyond iq: A triarchic theory of human intelligence.* Cambridge: Cambridge University Press.

Stojkovic, S., Kalinich, D., & Klofas, J. (1998). *Criminal justice organizations: Administration and management* (2nd ed.). Belmont, CA: Wadsworth Publishing.

Stubbs, E.C. (2005). Emotional intelligence competencies in the team and team leader: A multi-level examination of the impact of emotional intelligence on group performance. *Dissertation Abstracts International, 65,* 07A, 4663.

Terman, L.M. (1922). The great conspiracy or the impulse imperious of intelligence testers, psychoanalyzed and exposed by Mr. Lippmann. *New Republic,* 33, 116–120.

Terman, L.M., Otis, A.S., Dickson, V., Hubbard, O.S., Norton, J.K., Howard, L., et.al. (1917). A trial of mental and pedagogical test in a civil service examination for policemen and firemen. *Journal of Applied Psychology 21*, 1-2.

Tischler, L., Biberman, J., & McKeage, R. (2002). Linking emotional intelligence, spirituality and workplace performance: Definitions, models and ideas for research [Electronic edition]. *Journal of Managerial Psychology, 17*(3), 203-218.

Thorndike, E.L. (1920). Intelligence and its uses. *Harper's Magazine, 140*, 227-235.

Thorndike, R. (1994). Editorial. *Intelligence, 19*(2), 145-155.

Topping, K., Bremner, W., & Holmes, E.A. (2000). Social competence: The social construction of the concept. In R. Bar-On & J. D. A. Parker (Eds.), *The handbook of emotional intelligence: Theory, development, assessment, and application at home, school, and in the workplace* (pp. 28-39). San Francisco: Jossey-Bass.

Tower, G.M. (1988, September). Theories of multiple intelligence. *Gift of Fire*, 33. Retrieved March 3, 2005, from http://www.prometheussociety.org/articles/multiple.html.

Vitello-Cicciu, J.M. (2003). Emotional intelligence [Electronic edition]. *Nursing Management,* 29 – 33.

Vroom, V., & Yetton, P. (1973). *Leadership and decision making.* Pittsburgh, PA: University of Pittsburgh Press.

Walker, R.E., & Foley, J.M. (1973). Social intelligence: Its history and measurement. *Psychological Reports, 33*, 839-864.

Wechsler, D. (1974). *Selected papers of David Wechsler.* New York: Academic Press.

Wechsler, D. (1958). *The measurement and appraisal of adult intelligence.* Baltimore, MD: Williams and Wilkins.

Weinberger, L.A. (2003). An examination of the relationship between emotional intelligence, leadership style and perceived leadership effectiveness. *Dissertation Abstracts International, 64*, 11B. (UMI No. 3113218)

Westberg, E.M. (1931). A point of view: Studies in leadership. *Journal of Abnormal Social Psychology, 25*, 418-423.

Wheatley, M.J. (1999). *Leadership and the new science: Discovering order in a chaotic world.* San Francisco: Berrett-Koehler Publishers.

Whisenand, P.M., & Ferguson, R.F. (2002). *The managing of police organizations* (5th ed.). Upper Saddle River, NJ: Prentice Hall.

Williams, W.M., & Sternberg, R.J. (1988). Group intelligence: Why some groups are better than others [Electronic edition]. *Intelligence, 12,* 351-377.

Wong, C.S., & Law, K.S. (2002). The effects of leader and follower emotional intelligence on performance and attitude: An exploratory study [Electronic edition]. *The Leadership Quarterly, 13,* 243-274.

Yost, C.A., & Tucker, M.L. (2000). Are effective teams more emotionally intelligent? Confirming the importance of effective communication in teams [Electronic edition]. *Delta Pi Epsilon Journal, 42*(2), 101-109.

Zacker, J., & Bard, M. (1973). Effects of conflict management training on police performance. *Journal of Applied Psychology, 58*(2), 202-208.

Zirkel, S. (2000). Social intelligence: The development and maintenance of purposive behavior. In R. Bar-On & J. D. A. Parker (Eds.), *The handbook of emotional intelligence: Theory, development, assessment, and application at home, school, and in the workplace* (pp. 3-27). San Francisco: Jossey-Bass

127

APPENDICES

APPENDIX A

MODEL OF EMOTIONAL INTELLIGENCE

Emotional Self-Awareness: is the ability to recognize and understand one's feelings. It is not only the ability to be aware of one's feelings and emotions but also to differentiate between them, to know what one is feeling and why, and to know what caused the feelings.

Assertiveness: is the ability to express feelings, beliefs, and thoughts and defend one's rights in a nondestructive manner. Assertiveness is composed of three basic components: a0 the ability to express feelings, b) the ability to express beliefs and thoughts openly, and c) the ability to stand up for personal rights. Assertive people are not controlled or shy – they are able to outwardly express their feelings without being aggressive or abusive.

Self-Regard: is the ability to be aware of, understand, accept, and respect oneself. Respecting oneself essentially liking the way one exists. Self-acceptance is the ability to accept one's perceived positive and negative aspects as well as one's limitations and possibilities. This component of emotional intelligence is associated with general feelings of security, inner strength, self-assuredness, self-confidence, and feelings of self-adequacy. Feeling sure of oneself is dependent upon self-respect and self-esteem, which are based on a fairly well developed sense of identity.

Self-Actualization: is the ability to realize one's potential capacities and to strive to do that which one wants to do and enjoys doing. This component of emotional intelligence is manifested by the individual's becoming involved in pursuits that lead to a meaningful, rich, and full life. Striving to actualize one's potential involves developing enjoyable and meaningful activities and can mean a lifelong effort and an enthusiastic commitment to

long-term goals. Self-actualization is an ongoing, dynamic process of striving toward
maximum development of one's abilities, capacities, and talents.

Independence: is the ability to be self-directed in one's thinking, decisions, and actions
and to be free of emotional dependency. Independent people are self-reliant in planning
and making important decisions. They may, however, seek and consider other people's
opinions before making the right decision for themselves; consulting others is not
necessarily a sign of dependency. Independence is essentially the ability to function
autonomously versus needing protection and support – independent people avoid clinging
to others in order to satisfy their emotional needs.

Interpersonal Relationship: is the ability to establish and maintain mutually satisfying
relationships characterized by emotional closeness. Mutual satisfaction includes
meaningful social interchanges that are potentially rewarding and enjoyable. Positive
interpersonal relationship skill is characterized by the ability to give and receive warmth
and affection and to convey intimacy to another human being. This component is not
only associated with the desirability of cultivating friendly relations with others but with
the ability to feel at ease and comfortable in such relations and to possess positive
expectations concerning social intercourse.

Social Responsibility: is the ability to demonstrate oneself as a cooperative, contributing
and constructive member of one's social group. This ability involves acting in a
responsible manner, even though one may not benefit personally. Socially responsible
people have social consciousness and basic concern for others, which is manifested by
being able to take on community-oriented responsibilities. This component relates to the
ability to do things for and with others, accepting others, acting in accordance with one's
conscience, and upholding social roles. These people possess interpersonal sensitivity

and are able to accept others and use their talents for the good of the collective, not just the self.

Empathy: is the ability to be aware of, to understand, and to appreciate the feelings of others. It is "tuning in" to what, how, and why people feel the way they do. Being empathetic means being able to "emotionally read" other people. Empathetic people care about others and show interest in and concern for others.

Problem Solving: is the ability to identify and define problems as well as to generate and implement potentially effective solutions. Problem solving is multiphasic in nature and includes the ability to go through a process of a) sensing a problem and feeling confident and motivated to deal with it effectively, b) defining and formulating the problem as early as possible, c) generating as many solutions as possible, and d) making a decision to implement one of the solutions. Problem solving is associated with being conscientious, disciplined, methodical, and systematic in persevering and approaching problems. This skill is also linked to a desire to do one's best and to confront problems, rather than avoid them.

Reality Testing: is the ability to validate one's feelings by examining the correspondence between the subjective and the objective. Testing the degree of correspondence between what one experiences and what actually exists involves a search for objective evidence to confirm, justify, and support feelings, perceptions, and thoughts. Reality testing involves "tuning in" to the immediate situation, attempting to keep things in the correct perspective, and experiencing things as they really are, without excessive fantasizing or daydreaming about them. The emphasis is one of pragmatism, objectivity, the adequacy of one's perceptions, and authenticating one's ideas and thoughts.

Flexibility: is the ability to adjust one's emotions, thoughts, and behaviors to changing

situations and conditions. This component of emotional intelligence refers to one's

overall ability to adapt to unfamiliar, unpredictable, and dynamic circumstances. Flexible

people are agile, synergistic, and capable of reacting to change, without rigidity. These

people are able to change their minds when evidence suggests that they are mistaken.

They are generally open to and tolerant of different ideas, orientations, ways and

practices.

Stress Tolerance: is the ability to withstand adverse events, stressful situations, and

strong emotions without "falling apart" by actively coping with stress. It is the ability to

weather difficult situations without getting too overwhelmed. This ability is based on a)

a capacity to choose course of action for coping with stress, b) an optimistic disposition

toward new experiences and change in general and towards one's ability to successfully

overcome the specific problem at hand, and c) a feeling that one can control or influence

the stressful situation.

Impulse Control: is the ability to resist or delay an impulse, drive, or temptation to act

and to control one's emotions. It entails a capacity for accepting one's aggressive

impulses, being composed, and controlling aggression, hostility, and irresponsible

behavior.

Happiness (facilitator): is the ability to feel satisfied with one's life, to enjoy oneself and

being with others, and to have fun. Happiness combines self-satisfaction, general

contentment, and the ability to enjoy life. This component of emotional intelligence

involves the ability to enjoy various aspects of one's life and life in general. Happy

people often feel good and at ease in both work and leisure. Happiness is associated with

a general feeling of cheerfulness and enthusiasm. Happiness is a by-product and/or barometric indicator of one's overall degree of emotional intelligence and emotional functioning.

Optimism (facilitator): is the ability to look at the brighter side of life and to maintain a positive attitude, even in the face of adversity. Optimism assumes a measure of hope in one's approach to life. It is a positive approach to daily living.

Note. Acquired from Jaeger, 1999, Appendix A, pp. 181 – 183.

APPENDIX B

North Carolina State University is a land-grant university and a constituent institution of The University of North Carolina

Office of Research and Graduate Studies

NC STATE UNIVERSITY

Sponsored Programs and
Regulatory Compliance
Campus Box 7514
1 Leazar Hall
Raleigh, NC 27695-7514
919.515.7200
919.515.7721 (fax)

From: Debra A. Paxton, IRB Administrator
North Carolina State University
Institutional Review Board

Date: June 31, 2005

Project Title: The Relationship Between Emotional Intelligence of Patrol Supervisors and Subordinate Patrol Officers

IRB#:   159-05-6

Dear Mr. Burnette:

The project listed above has been reviewed in accordance with expedited review procedures under Addendum 46 FR8392 of 45 CFR 46 and is approved for one year. **This protocol expires on June 31, 2006, and will need continuing review before that date.**

NOTE:

1.   This board complies with requirements found in Title 45 part 46 of The Code of Federal Regulations. For NCSU the Assurance Number is: FWA00003429; the IRB Number is: IRB00000330.

2.   The IRB must be notified of any changes that are made to this study.

3.   Your approval for this study lasts for one year from the review date. If your study extends beyond that time, including data analysis, you must obtain continuing review from the IRB.

Please provide your faculty sponsor with a copy of this letter. Thank you.

Sincerely,

Debra Paxton
NCSU IRB

134

APPENDIX C

Dear Sergeant or Officer _____,

Greetings. My name is Mike Burnette and I am presently engaged in a doctoral dissertation project at North Carolina State University (NCSU). I am a former law enforcement officer and currently I am serving as a Magistrate in Swain County. I also chair the Criminal Justice / Cyber Crime Department at Southwestern Community College.

The purpose in writing this letter is to request your participation in my dissertation project. I am researching the correlational relationship of emotional intelligence levels of patrol sergeants and the respective officers that they supervise.

I realize that you are very busy with many occupational and family obligations and with that acknowledgement I am requesting a very short-term commitment of less than one hour of your time to complete online the Emotional Quotient Inventory (EQ-i) and a demographic questionnaire. The EQ-i consists of 125 questions and the demographic consists of fewer than ten questions.

As indicated in the attached *Consent to Participate* document, your personal information and identity will be vigorously guarded and maintained by me and disclosure of your personal information and assessment results will never occur to anyone else or to any agency or organization without your expressed, written authorization.

I hope that you will join with me in this important research work and participate in this study. If you have any questions regarding this study, please feel free to contact me (828) 488-9315 or (828) 508-5767. Please feel free to visit my homepage at Southwestern Community College at http://www.southwesterncc.edu/mikeb/profile.htm to find out more about me. I would also encourage you to contact your fellow officers and sergeants in the Western North Carolina area for their recommendations as well.

If you agree to participate, I would ask that you respond to me by email on or before July 26, 2005. Upon receiving the email acknowledgment of your participation in the study, I will email to you a unique identifier code and access information to complete the inventory and questionnaire.

Thank you for your consideration and I look forward to working with you on this research project.

Fraternally,

Michael E. Burnette

APPENDIX D

CONSENT TO PARTICIPATE

I.   You are being invited to participate in a dissertation study conducted by Michael E. Burnette, a doctoral candidate at North Carolina State University, Raleigh, NC. This study is an independent project created and funded entirely by Mr. Burnette. Your agency has not solicited or requested that this project be implemented by the researcher; however, the Commander of your agency is supportive of the overall research opportunity provided by this study. The purpose of this study is to explore the relationship between the emotional intelligence levels of line sergeants and their respective subordinate officers. It is hoped that the information obtained will contribute to the understanding of emotional intelligence within the policing profession.

II.   Participation in this study is completely voluntary. You may refuse to participate or withdraw from the study, at any time, without penalty or negative repercussions. If you agree to participate, you will be asked to complete the following:
a. An assessment measurement of emotional intelligence
b. A demographic profile
Both of these items will be accessible in a secure online format that will require less than one hour of time to complete.

III.   In order to protect your private information from being disclosed in any manner, a unique identifier code will be assigned to you that you may use to access the online test and demographic profile. The information regarding your personal information will only be accessible by the researcher who will be responsible for supplying you with the unique identifier code. Members of your department **will not** be allowed to see any of the information that you provide or the results of any assessment measures that you complete.

IV.   The results of your EQ-i assessment may be shared with Dr. Reuven Bar-On, author of the EQ-i test, as well as the test publisher, Multi-Health Systems (MHS). The purpose of sharing this information is to contribute to the further development of the EQ-i test. Your identity will be protected, as neither your name nor the location of your department will be disclosed at any time to anyone. You maintain the right to either refuse to participate or request that your results be withheld from Dr. Bar-On or MHS.

V.   If, at any time, you have questions about the research project, you may contact Mike Burnette, the principal researcher, at (828) 488-9315 or (828) 508-5767.

APPENDIX E

Consent Form

I have read the consent to participate information regarding the research project entitled *Relationship Between Emotional Intelligence in Patrol Sergeants and Subordinate Patrol Officers* being conducted by Michael E. Burnette, doctoral candidate at NCSU and primary researcher.

I understand that by responding to the researcher's initial email message that I am implying my consent to participate in this study. I will acknowledge my agreement to participate in this study by sending an email message that states that I agree to participate in this study.

I also understand that my personal information and assessment results will be maintained by the researcher and will not be disclosed to any person, agency, or organization without my expressed, written authorization.

[Please print or save a copy of this document as an acknowledgement of your consent]

APPENDIX F

Sergeant or Officer,

Please follow the instructions listed in both of the following steps:

Step 1:

You are being asked to complete the BarOn EQ-i (125). Please visit <u>Bar-On's Emotional Quotient Inventory (EQ-i)</u> and login with the code and password that appear below.

Code: 3242-001-***
Password: *****

Instructions for how to complete the BarOn EQ-i (125) will appear once you have logged in.

If you have any questions or concerns about completing this questionnaire, please feel free to contact me by email at <u>mikeb@southwest.cc.nc.us</u> or by telephone at (828) 488-9315 or (828) 508-5767. Thank you for your cooperation.

Step 2:

Please visit the <u>Sergeant's Demographic Profile</u> or <u>Officer's Demographic Profile</u> and complete the nine questions presented in this survey.

I have also attached a Word document that allows you to go directly to the websites by clicking on the hyperlinks.

These websites may be accessed at any computer with internet access at any time - day or night.

Thank you for your assistance in this endeavor,

Fraternally,

Mike Burnette

APPENDIX G

Sergeant's Demographic Profile

1. Please indicate your unique identifier here.

   _____

2. Please indicate your total number of years as a line sergeant.

   _____

3. Please indicate your total number of years in service with your current agency.

   _____

4. Please indicate your current geographic duty assignment, based upon these descriptions.

   ☐ a. Rural, Small Population County (Under 50,000)
   ☐ b. Rural, Medium Population County (Greater than 50,000, Less than 100,000)
   ☐ c. Large Population County (Greater than 100,000)
   ☐ d. Urban City Environment
   ☐ e. Metropolitan City Environment

5. Please indicate the number of years that you have supervised your current group of officers.

   _____

6. Please indicate your current educational credentials (highest level).

   ☐ a. GED or High School Diploma
   ☐ b. Some college
   ☐ c. Associate's Degree
   ☐ d. Bachelor's Degree
   ☐ e. Master's Degree
   ☐ f. Doctoral Degree

7. Please indicate the total number of years of previous law enforcement supervisory experience that you had prior to joining your current agency.

_____

8. Having just completed Bar-On's Emotional Quotient Inventory (EQ-i), how would you rate your emotional intelligence level?

Needing Improvement	Functionally Effective	Highly Effective
☐	☐	☐

9. How would you rank the emotional intelligence level of your subordinate officers as a collective group?

Needing Improvement	Functionally Effective	Highly Effective
☐	☐	☐

140

APPENDIX H

Officer's Demographic Profile

1. Please indicate your unique identifier here.

    _____

2. Please indicate your total number of years as an officer.

    _____

3. Please indicate your total number of years in service with your current agency.

    _____

4. Please indicate your current geographic duty assignment, based upon these descriptions.

    ☐ a. Rural, Small Population County (Under 50,000)
    ☐ b. Rural, Medium Population County (Greater than 50,000, Less than 100,000)
    ☐ c. Large Population County (Greater than 100,000)
    ☐ d. Urban City Environment
    ☐ e. Metropolitan City Environment

5. Please indicate the number of years that you have supervised by your current sergeant.

    _____

6. Please indicate your current educational credentials (highest level).

    ☐ a. GED or High School Diploma
    ☐ b. Some college
    ☐ c. Associate's Degree
    ☐ d. Bachelor's Degree
    ☐ e. Master's Degree
    ☐ f. Doctoral Degree

7. Please indicate the total number of years of previous law enforcement experience that you had prior to joining your current agency.

    _____

8. Having just completed Bar-On's Emotional Quotient Inventory (EQ-i), how would you rate your emotional intelligence level?

Needing Improvement	Functionally Effective	Highly Effective
☐	☐	☐

9. How would you rank the emotional intelligence level of your supervising sergeant?

Needing Improvement	Functionally Effective	Highly Effective
☐	☐	☐

APPENDIX I

Sergeant or Officer,

This letter is written to serve the purpose of providing feedback to you regarding the Emotional Quotient Inventory (EQ-i) test that you participated in as part of a doctoral dissertation project that I am conducting through North Carolina State University and to also thank you for your assistance in completing this project.

I am including in this email to you the following attachments: 1) Your individual EQ-i test results in a .pdf format, 2) A Model of Emotional Intelligence that outlines a brief explanation of each of the 15 subscales of Emotional Intelligence in a Word .doc format, and 3) A Chart representing the Interpretative Guidelines for EQ-i scores in a Word .doc format. I believe that you will be able to easily discern your scores and interpret the results based upon these three attachments.

If you should have any additional questions or concerns, I would be happy to talk with you at any time. My contact information is as follows: (800) 447-4091 x 276 (office) at SCC, (828) 488-9315 (home) or (828) 508-5767 (cell). My email address is mikeb@southwest.cc.nc.us.

Dr. ****** ******, Industrial Psychologist for your agency has offered his/her services to any of you that would like to talk with him/her regarding this test. His/her telephone number is (***) ***-**** and his/her email is ********@*****. You may share your individual test results with Dr. ****** if you would like; however, if you wish for me to provide your EQ-i results to Dr. ****** or any other person, it will be necessary to provide me a signed statement indicating your desire for me to share that information with a third party.

I wish to thank you for your tremendous contribution to assisting me in completing this project and also special thanks from the law enforcement community as a collective group for the valuable data garnered from your participation. Your participation has also provided a significant benefit to the research literature available in this career field.

Thank you again for all of your help and support!

Fraternally,

Mike Burnette

LaVergne, TN USA
20 July 2010

190158LV00006B/1/A

9 783836 434737